'97
op

5⁰⁰

9/83

80

LIVING IN CITIES

By the same author

An Illustrated History of Transportation

ANTHONY RIDLEY

LIVING IN CITIES

THE JOHN DAY COMPANY   NEW YORK

The John Day Company, 257 Park Avenue South, New York, N.Y. 10010 an Intext publisher

Library of Congress Catalog Card Number: 73-150961
Printed in the United States of America

Contents

I

The First Cities

Fifty-five hundred years ago the Sumerians became the first men to live in cities. Temples, palaces, and humble mud-brick houses rose above the land of Mesopotamia, which lay between the twin rivers Tigris and Euphrates. For the first time men experienced the pleasures and problems of living close together in a man-made environment.

Like all other peoples who have since learned to build towns, the Sumerians were successful farmers. Populous cities cannot survive without an assured food supply, and the art of farming, which was first mastered in the Middle East, had to spread or be learned anew before cities could evolve in other regions of the world. Agriculture is perhaps the most important discovery ever made.

Almost certainly women were the earliest farmers. Stone Age men had nothing to do with plants. They hunted and fished while their wives were relegated to searching for edible fruits and vegetables. In the Middle East women often collected the nourishing seeds of the wild wheat and barley native to that area.

Over the generations it was noticed how seeds germinated, and about 12,000 years ago a few women began to risk part of their precious store of food in an attempt to grow crops in places of their own choosing. The success of their experiments changed the whole history of mankind.

Other women became cultivators, while their husbands learned to tame the wild goats, sheep, and cattle they had formerly hunted. Men no longer wandered in pursuit of herds of game, but settled in well-watered areas, tilled their fields, and gathered in their harvest of cereals. Small, permanent villages began to appear in the fertile hill country of the Middle East. One of the earliest yet discovered was at Jarmo in Iraq, where in about 7000 B.C. the inhabitants grew both wheat and barley, and raised goats and possibly cattle as well.

For thousands of years the agricultural villages prospered peacefully.

There was little cause for conflict. In most areas there was still plenty of free land, so if a local population became too large some of the families could easily move away to found a new settlement. Villages seldom rose above a few hundred inhabitants.

In drier regions, however, a new pattern was being set for the future. People were loath to leave even a crowded desert oasis, and were also prepared to defend it against intruders. By about 7000 B.C. the oasis settlement of Jericho in Jordan contained perhaps two thousand people living within a stone wall which enclosed ten acres. Jericho was still a collection of individual farmers rather than a town community, but its need for defence foreshadowed the events which were to bring true cities into existence.

As the centuries rolled by, farmers became so skilful that they grew more grain than their own families could eat. It was no longer necessary for everyone to labour on the land. A few men could develop specialized crafts, and supply their neighbours with pots or stone tools in exchange for food. The village could also support a far more important craftsman, the magician, without whose good offices the harvest would certainly fail. From practitioners of crude magic the medicine men evolved into a priestly caste dedicated to the service of agricultural gods. Holy places were set aside and formal religion began.

Agricultural success eventually produced a great increase in population. Unoccupied fertile land grew steadily more difficult to find and so territorial disputes increased in frequency and violence. The situation was at its worse on the Mesopotamian plain where the scanty rainfall made irrigation by river water a necessity for efficient farming. The two great rivers, Euphrates and Tigris, were vital to the existence of the expanding population, so that communities guarded their access to the river banks with jealous fury. Infringements of water rights brought savage reprisals. Warfare seemed ceaseless.

Often a successful war chief, who had the acclaim of grateful neighbours and the support of the young warriors, clung to power even when victory was finally won. As gratitude soured, the chieftain had to employ his strength to coerce and control the very people he had formerly protected. The saviour had become the despot.

Such a ruler searching for a fortified camp from which his soldiers could terrorize the surrounding countryside, would think naturally of the shrine or holy place where local religious feeling was focused. Control of this centre would give him sacred as well as secular prestige.

2   Chief and priest became partners. Temporal power received divine

Modern Erbil squatting on the ancient city mound of Arbela, Iraq, gives an idea of the appearance of a Sumerian city.

sanction, and the idea of kingship was born. Subjects were no longer required to obey a mere man. In future they were to bow down to the representative of the gods to whom everything ultimately belonged.

The sacred citadel of the king acted as a magnet drawing people out of their isolated villages and clustering them close under the security of its walls. Here was where they were safest from enemy raids; where they could best serve the will of the gods; where action and excitement were centred. More and more sprang up around the original holy ground, which by now was adorned with temples and palaces. Peasants became citizens united by the common aim of serving the gods through obedience to their intermediaries, the king and the priests. Strife and kingship had produced politically united settlements dwarfing anything which had preceded them. The ancient Sumerian inhabitants of Mesopotamia had 3

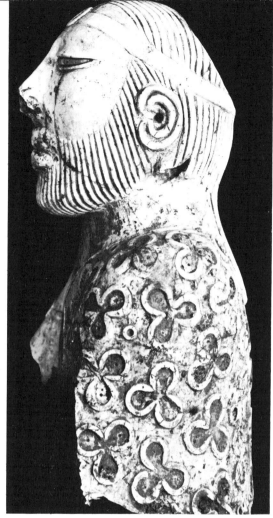

Statuette of an ancient Sumerian
townsman found in a city mound.

Head of a man from Mohenjo-daro in
the Indus valley.

invented the city.

By about 3000 B.C. numerous high-walled cities rose along the banks of
the lower reaches of the Euphrates and Tigris. Most had their own king
or "lugal," which in the Sumerian language meant "big man." Each "big
man" wanted to be bigger still, and cities like Uruk, Ur, Lagash, Umma,
and Kish strove and plotted against one another in a quest for political
domination. It was a dangerous world where a city's walls had to be
strong and its citizens united.

Within the city walls life was controlled by a civil service of priests.
The temple was a hive of industry as well as a religious centre. Ordinary
citizens were still sent out to tend the fields which surrounded the city,
but the artisans stayed in town. Each of the craftsmen had his allotted
place in a temple workshop, where he was provided with raw materials

4

Reconstruction of the ziggurat at Ur.

and given his task for the day. Potters, weavers, and metal workers all practised their skills under the direction of the priests. The products of both field and workshop flowed into the many warehouses ranged about the temples, and workmen were paid in issues of food from the communal store. By about 3000 B.C. the transactions had become so complex that the Sumerian priests were forced to invent a form of writing to keep a check on the goods which passed through their hands.

Sumerian cities with their encircling walls, dominant temples, mud-brick buildings, and unplanned streets are so similar that a description of one gives a good picture of all. The city of Ur, at the close of the third millennium B.C., squatted on a low hill of its own making. For fifteen hundred years new buildings had mounted on the ruins of old until the city had risen clear of the often flooded plain below. A huge rampart, seventy-seven feet thick at the base, supported the man-made mound, and served as the foundation for a fortified wall which encircled the whole city. Twenty thousand people lived in the mud-brick houses that crammed the 150 acres enclosed by the defences. The city was a maze of narrow, winding alleys, and only a few important streets were wide enough for wheeled traffic.

At the core of the city was its administrative and temple area, raised on a platform well above the general level. Here were the city's only open spaces, and here its monumental buildings. The ziggurat, a brick hill erected in honour of the gods, dwarfed everything else. Its rectangular base, 200 feet long and 150 feet wide, was surmounted by successively smaller stages until the whole massive structure towered up to 70 feet. On the summit was a small shrine reached by a splendid processional staircase. In front of the ziggurat was a paved court 90 yards wide, while flanking it were the temples, workshops, and storehouses where most of the city's business was transacted.

5

The cities of Sumer may well have been matched by equally ancient towns in Egypt. It is hard to be sure. Most early Egyptian settlements have long since disappeared beneath silt from the flooding Nile, and even those few which stood high enough to avoid burial have been systematically pillaged by modern peasants eager to crumble the age-old bricks into fertilizer.

Although the evidence of ruins is lacking, there are other hints as to the antiquity of Egyptian cities. Later Egyptian literature has preserved the names of several city-states which are supposed to have flourished in the Nile Delta long before the semi-legendary conqueror, Menes, united

Symbolic pictures of Egyptian walled towns on a piece of carved stone dating from about 3200 B.C.

the whole country under his rule in about 3200 B.C. Written tradition has been supported by the discovery of a fourth millennium B.C. Egyptian slate palette, which was inscribed with symbolic pictures of what were clearly walled cities. In the present state of knowledge it is probably better to grant priority to Sumerian cities, but Egypt could not have been far behind.

Just before its unification Egypt had already progressed to the point where there were only two powers in the land. In the north the Delta people looked to the city of Wazet for leadership, while in the south the towns of the upper Nile accepted as joint capitals the twin cities of Nekheb and Nekhen, which faced one another across the river. When Menes led the southern armies into the Delta and overthrew its league of cities, nothing stood between him and complete sovereignty.

6

To cement his hold over the country Menes built the walled city of Memphis commanding the apex of the Delta. In time, Memphis, which is a few miles south of modern Cairo, grew into one of Egypt's most powerful and prosperous cities, and from 2780 to 2258 B.C. was capital of the whole kingdom.

Memphis was a typical Egyptian city. It contained impressive temples, but as in Sumerian cities, houses, workshops, and wharves were jumbled together without any planning, along narrow, crooked alleys. No secular structure was built to last. Mud and wood were considered good enough to fashion the dwellings of the living. Stone, on the other hand, was reserved for the tombs of the dead and the temples of the gods. Thus, the Egyptians, with their strong belief in the supernatural and the afterlife, devoted their architectural skill to their sacred buildings.

Farming, cities, and civilization were born in the Middle East, but eventually other peoples learned the same skills. Agriculture spread from its original centre into India and Europe, but was possibly discovered independently in the more distant China. The Western hemisphere, which was cut off from the influence of the Old World, had to develop the art of cultivation by itself. As farming became established in new regions, it was only a matter of time before cities grew up all over the world.

By 3000 B.C. agriculture was already highly developed throughout the one-thousand-mile-long Indus Valley in what is now Pakistan. Farming villages grew into towns, and from about 2300 to 1750 B.C. many proud cities rose beside the Indus and its tributaries. The character of these towns was very different from those of Mesopotamia. Instead of jumble and filth there were order and cleanliness; instead of building massive walls like those which ringed the cities of Sumer, the less warlike Indus people preferred to concentrate their defences on an inner citadel.

Like all other Indus cities the two largest, Mohenjo-daro and Harappā, were built of long-lasting baked bricks. Unfortunately Harappā was ransacked for ballast by nineteenth-century railway contractors; but Mohenjo-daro is still well preserved. Excavations have revealed that the city was dominated by a walled enclosure perched on an artificial mound some 50 feet high. Secure within this raised citadel stood Mohenjo-daro's public buildings. The huge communal granary is easily recognized, but the purpose of the other structures is open to dispute. Probably they, like the great water tank which was also sheltered within the fortifications, had some religious use.

7

A narrow alley in Mohenjo-daro.

Beneath the frowning walls of the citadel, the neatly laid out city occupied about one square mile. Several wide main roads intersecting at right angles cut the town into a number of rectangular districts, each some twelve hundred feet long and six hundred feet wide. Side streets and alleys running off the main roads were very narrow, but they too were straight and conformed to the overall grid pattern. Although none of the streets was paved, there was an excellent drainage system and houses were even supplied with brick refuse bins. The gaunt ruins of the once splendid city still convey a sense of its original planning and civic pride.

Of the great ancient civilizations of the Old World, China was the last to produce cities. Agriculture was practised from about seven thousand years ago, but as late as 2000 B.C. the largest settlements were still villages surrounded by simple mud walls. According to Chinese tradition it was about then that a single ruler united the Yellow River region under his control. Certainly, communities grew in size during the first part of the second millennium B.C., and by the time the first fully historical dynasty, the Shang, came to power around 1500 B.C., Chinese cities had finally emerged. Legend speaks of the Shang princes overthrowing eighteen hundred city-states, which even allowing for exaggeration suggests a very sizable urban population.

Little is known about the earliest Chinese towns, but Anyang, which was capital from c. 1300 to c. 1000 B.C., has been excavated. It was surrounded by a wall of rammed earth with watch towers built at intervals along its length. Inside the wall even important buildings were made from the simplest of materials. Wood and thatch provided shelter for noble and commoner alike.

Far away in the isolated New World most of the Indians of the North remained hunters and food gatherers, but in South and Central America people evolved their own unique form of agriculture. Mexico, where cultivation started around 5000 B.C., needed two thousand years of slowly accumulating experience before the first permanent farming villages could take root. Once the villages were established and prospering, a priestly caste emerged and gradually assumed increasing power. By the first millennium B.C. the priests had gathered enough authority to order the construction of impressive centres of worship. Stone was quarried, transported, carved into idols, fashioned into altars, and built into huge, flat-topped pyramids. Majestic shrines were raised to the gods. Village people flocked to such centres for religious festivals, but once the ceremonies were over they went home. Such sacred cities as La Venta and San Lorenzo, despite their monumental architecture, had virtually no permanent populations.

The first and greatest of pre-Columbian cities, Teotihuacán in central Mexico, was founded at the beginning of the Christian era. By about A.D. 400, when it reached the height of its power, the vast city covered eight 9

Teotihuacán from the air looking to the southeast. The huge pyramids once dominated a bustling city.

square miles and had between fifty- and a hundred-thousand inhabitants.

Teotihuacán's chief feature was its spaciousness. A superb, broad avenue ran from south to north, cleaving the city in half before halting at the base of a towering pyramid. To the east an even more majestic pyramid, with a height of 210 feet and a base area of more than 12 acres, rose from amongst the hundred or more temples which flanked the ceremonial way. At the heart of the city a great temple lay east of the main avenue, while, on the opposite side of the road, buildings were clustered around what might have been a market square. A second wide street, at right angles to the first, extended for two miles on either side of this twin centre of the city. All subsidiary roads were arranged to fit a strict grid pattern, and ran parallel to one or another of the major highways.

These then were some of the world's earliest cities — very different in form but linked by their common reliance on successful farming. Without the backing of agriculture cities cannot exist, just as without the stimulus of city life advanced civilization is impossible. The whole progress of mankind has stemmed from the discovery of farming and the development of cities.

2

The Townsman's Home

Houses take shape and form in response to the problems which every city environment sets its inhabitants. Townsmen of succeeding civilizations have used their varying resources of materials and skill to suit their homes, as best they could, to the prevailing climate and the available space. Many different designs have evolved, and living standards have risen and fallen as civilizations have waxed and waned. There has been no steady progress. Sometimes, in fact, conditions have worsened sharply. Housing in Imperial Rome, for all its deficiencies, was superior to anything in the cities of medieval Europe, while even today many Indian townspeople would envy the order and cleanliness of Mohenjo-daro four thousand years ago.

The first cities grew up in the hot, almost treeless mud-land of Meso-potamia, where wood was so expensive that its use had to be kept to a minimum. Mud and reeds were the only materials which the Sumerians possessed in abundance, and these they used to construct their cities. House walls were made of mud-brick, while roofing was provided by mud-daubed reeds. The design favoured by Sumerian builders was well adapted to the climate. Rooms were clustered around an inner courtyard onto which all the windows opened. Blank outer walls kept out the fierce glare of the sun, and ensured privacy in the crowded cities.

The middle-class homes of the early second millennium B.C., excavated at Ur by Sir Leonard Woolley, were of this traditional, inward looking type. Although only the lower courses of brick survived, ruined internal staircases suggested that the houses had originally stood two storeys high. Further evidence of this was provided by one building in which traces of a supporting post convinced the archaeologists that a wooden gallery had once jutted out over the courtyard to give access from the head of the stairs to the upper rooms. No sleeping apartments were identified amongst the long, narrow ground floor rooms, so it was supposed that the family slept upstairs. The typical ground floor contained a kitchen, a large room

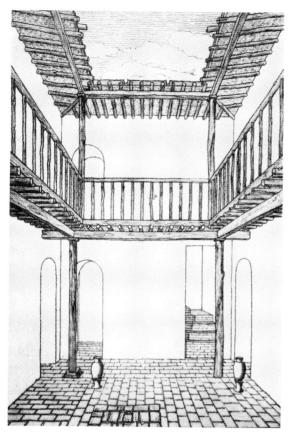

Restoration of a house at Ur dating
from about 1800 B.C.

for receiving guests, servants' quarters, and often a private chapel below
which the ancestors were buried. There was also a lavatory discreetly
tucked away behind the stairs. In all, making a guess for the upper floor,
each house probably consisted of thirteen or fourteen rooms. The Sumerian
middle class lived in style.

The physical environment of the Indus Valley was not dissimilar to
that of Mesopotamia, and although the open cities of the peaceable Indus
people were in sharp contrast to the closely walled towns of war-torn
Sumer, the actual houses of the two civilizations had much in common.
At Mohenjo-daro and other cities of the Indus Valley houses of about the
same antiquity and status as those at Ur again consisted of rooms ranged
around an inner courtyard. Often stairs led up to a second storey, and the
more fortunate dwellings boasted bathrooms and water-flushed lavatories
as well. Conditions were not so good for ordinary workmen, however.
Their small, brick-built homes, each with only two rooms and a tiny
courtyard, were squeezed tightly together in monotonous rows. Even in
2000 B.C. there were painful differences in the living standards of rich and
poor within the same city.

On island Crete the Minoan civilization, which also flourished during

Minoan town houses.

the second millennium B.C., built cities in a very different setting. The climate was mild, and the Minoans, far from wishing to exclude the sunlight, welcomed it. Although their great palaces were built around courtyards, their private houses were rectangular structures, well supplied with windows.

A vivid impression of these Minoan town houses can still be gained from pictures on a number of porcelain plaques found amongst the ruins of the palace of Knossos. Each plaque depicted a separate, rectangular, flat-roofed building rising to two or sometimes three storeys. In most houses the only opening at street level was the door, indicating perhaps that the ground floor was used as a storage basement. Above, an array of windows let a flood of light into the upper rooms. The Minoans' obvious pleasure in brightness, and the traces of paint which remain on the plaques strongly suggest that the walls of the houses were brilliantly coloured. A Minoan town in its heyday must have looked as gay as a modern Mediterranean resort.

Contact with Crete did much to encourage the rise of civilization in mainland Greece, but the Greeks never absorbed the Minoan interest in domestic architecture. Public affairs were more important to the Greeks than private life. They were eager to participate in running their city, to meet in the assembly, to exercise in the gymnasium, and to walk and talk with their friends in public places. They were not anxious to sit idly at home. Most of their exceptional artistic skill was lavished on temples and other civic buildings, which added to the dignity of their city. Little thought was wasted on mere homes, and in many of the greatest towns of classical Greece the houses were little better than hovels. In the fifth century B.C. the superb Acropolis of Athens dominated a congested city of narrow, stinking streets, whose closely packed houses were built around diminutive courtyards. Sanitation was more or less lacking. Although the Greeks were in most ways a very advanced people, housing standards had taken a step backwards from the time of Minos.

13

Model of Roman flats at the port of Ostia.

The buildings of Imperial Rome, the greatest Western city before the beginnings of industrialization, were mainly a response to the problem of housing a huge population in a limited space. At the peak of its power in the second century A.D. Rome's inhabitants numbered a million, but the built-up area never exceeded eight square miles. There was no public transport, so the city had to stay compact if it were to keep its suburbs within easy walking distance of the centre. This could only be done by expanding upwards, and Rome learned to build higher than any city had ever done before. By the close of the third century A.D. Rome had over 46,000 tall blocks of flats, the so called "insulae" or "islands," but less than 2,000 private houses.

Tall buildings were already common in the time of the first Emperor, Augustus, who lived from 63 B.C. to A.D. 14. The builders of his reign, however, often allowed their confidence to outgrow their skill, and not infrequently the rumble of a collapsing block echoed through the city. To prevent further disasters Augustus forbade any private contractor to build higher than sixty-five feet, but in this matter even imperial power was forced occasionally to bow to necessity. If the people were to be housed, tall buildings were essential. The Insula of Felicula, built about A.D. 200, most certainly flouted all height regulations. A veritable skyscraper, it towered so high over the surrounding five-storey blocks that it became famous throughout the whole Roman world.

Externally, Rome's giant blocks of flats would not have looked too out of place in a modern city. Windows were large, and window-boxes of flowers common; elegant facings disguised the fragility of the walls, and shops often occupied the ground floors. But inside, the tenements presented a different picture. The large windows were open to the elements, because although the Romans knew of glass panes only the rich could afford to use them. Flat dwellers kept out the cold or wet only at the expense of excluding the daylight with wooden shutters. To make things even more miserable there was neither a fireplace nor the hypocaust under-floor heating enjoyed by the wealthy. In severe weather the only source of comfort was the pitifully inadequate open charcoal brazier around which the family would hunch in the thickest clothing they could muster.

Sanitary arrangements in the tenements were just as bad. As far as is known none of the upper storeys was ever connected to Rome's justly famous sewer system. Instead buckets were either brought down and emptied into a vat at the bottom of the stairs or surreptitiously discharged out of a window at night. Rome's narrow alleys were dangerous places after dusk.

Aqueducts poured water into Rome in unprecedented volumes, but none flowed directly into the tenements. Only the rich could afford the privilege of pipes laid on their homes, and the flat dwellers had to fetch their water from a public fountain and then cart it all the way upstairs. The ordinary people of the most powerful city of its time were wretchedly housed despite the imposing appearance of the "insulae" in which they lived.

A little silk and a few vague stories were all that reached Rome from another great civilization far away to the east. At the beginning of the Christian era China was controlled by the Han dynasty, which ruled over about fifty million subjects. Even in those early times perhaps as much as a third of the population lived in towns. Some of the cities were very large. Ch'ang-an, the capital from 202 B.C. to A.D. 8, had over 200,000 inhabitants protected by an encircling wall twenty-five kilometres in perimeter. This provided an enclosed area twice as great as that of Rome in which to house a much smaller population. Space was never a problem in Ch'ang-an, and most houses remained the same simple thatch, wattle, and daub cottages that had served country people for centuries. Only the rich built distinctive, multi-storey town houses, which were reinforced with timber frames and roofed with tiles.

Early in the third century A.D. the Han dynasty was overthrown and barbarians seized the northern regions of the empire. A troubled period of disunity, during which town life must have suffered, lasted for nearly four hundred years.

Rome too eventually succumbed to difficulties. A gradual shift of political influence to the rich and prosperous eastern provinces forced the Emperor Constantine to move the seat of government. In A.D. 330 his new city of Constantinople, founded on the previous town of Byzantium, became the official capital of the empire. Rome declined and during the fifth century A.D. was sacked several times by marauding barbarians. Roman power in western Europe collapsed, leaving the towns it had fostered to dwindle into shadows of their former selves. Cities and civilization were almost lost to Europe, but the urban way of life continued in the Eastern Roman Empire, dominated by Constantinople.

In some ways Constantinople was an echo of the former capital. The private houses of the wealthy were again few in number, but those which did exist were extremely comfortable. Glass windows and hypocaust heating kept at least some rooms warm and snug in winter, while the balconies, roof gardens, and inner courtyards made the houses delightful when the sun shone.

A large proportion of the population, however, lived crowded together in towering blocks of flats just as their Roman predecessors had done. If anything, the Byzantine tenements were higher, some reaching nine storeys, so that life for many must have seemed an endless trudge up and down the stairs.

But even the top floor tenants were well off compared with the squatters. In common with many South American and Asian cities today, Constantinople faced the problem of peasants flooding into the city to build miserable shacks on whatever open ground they could find. Colonies of rush-roofed huts sprang up overnight, often around the most famous buildings in the city. The authorities seemed powerless to help or hinder, and the question of how squatters should be controlled remained unanswered right up to the final conquest of Constantinople by the Turks in 1453.

In the fifth century, when the Western Roman Empire collapsed, Constantinople had about 500,000 inhabitants. As western towns shrank, Constantinople grew. By the ninth century most European settlements were no more than a scattering of huts ringed by a wall or palisade to keep out marauders, but in the East nearly a million people lived securely behind the huge fortifications of Constantinople. Although town life began to pick up again in the West during the eleventh century, it was 1200 before even the largest of its cities, Paris, approached a quarter of the size

HIC:EST:VVAD ARD:

Peasants' huts, a scene from the Bayeux Tapestry.

of the great eastern capital. To the very end of the medieval period most western towns remained small. Many had populations below a thousand, and the few, which like Venice and Paris exceeded 100,000 inhabitants, were considered marvels of the age.

Until the thirteenth century the homes of all but the richest of medieval townsmen were humble shelters lacking in nearly every comfort. The general absence of security did not encourage elaborate buildings. Three typical cottages of the early Middle Ages are shown on the Bayeux Tapestry, which was made a few years after the Norman conquest of England in 1066. Two had walls made of horizontal, overlapping planks, but one seems to have been made from stone blocks. The wooden shingle or possibly slate roofs were unbroken by any opening, so the rude, single-storey huts probably lacked even the luxury of a fire in winter. There were no windows, just a single low doorway for each house. Home life could have held few attractions in those days.

Even the houses of wealthier people offered little ease or privacy. Often the entire household shared one large, single room — the hall, which, to give some security against surprise attack, was built above a ground floor storeroom and approached only by an easily defended external staircase. King Harold's manor, also shown in the Bayeux Tapestry, was a house of this kind.

Housing improved during the thirteenth and fourteenth centuries though it was often very primitive by modern standards. The poorer townsmen still generally lived in thatched or shingle-roofed wooden huts packed close together along unpaved alleys into which all the household filth was thrown. Conditions were better for the successful tradesman. He lived with his family and apprentices in a two-storey house of timber-framed construction, which combined living quarters with shop and factory. The ground floor was given over to commerce. Goods made in the workroom at the rear were sold in a shop at the front. When work was done for the day the family and its retainers withdrew upstairs to domestic quarters, often consisting of nothing more than a living-room and a single bedroom. Originally, entry to the upper storey was by means of a ladder that was pulled up as soon as all were safely in for the night, but as time went on it became increasingly common to install permanent staircases.

Medieval building plots had a small frontage, but stretched back some way from the street. To make the most of their sites, long, narrow houses were built with roofs rising from common dividing walls and with gable ends facing the road. Behind were gardens cluttered with outbuildings, which often sheltered cattle or pigs. As late as the sixteenth century the majority of German townsmen kept a cow or at least a few pigs in their yards.

During the winter even the better medieval houses must have been as oppressively dark and smoky. Glass was too expensive for domestic window panes until the fifteenth century, and although slices of horn or oiled cloth were sometimes used, most people kept out both the inclement weather and the daylight by closing wooden shutters. Only the communal living-room was heated, and until the end of the thirteenth century there were no chimneys, so that smoke from the open fire had to find its way out through a hole in the roof.

However, it would be wrong to paint too black a picture of conditions in medieval towns. People had plenty of free time in which to escape from dark workrooms and narrow, overhung streets into the gardens and open spaces behind the houses. Also, even if the stench of garbage at times became unbearable, nearly all medieval towns were small, so relief could easily be found in the fresh air of the countryside. Most important of all, inside their encircling wall townsmen were free, at a time when most peasants were serfs bound to the land of tyrannical masters.

By the fifteenth century, when space within town walls was already becoming limited, the wealthier citizens were building higher, and their timber-framed houses stretched up to three storeys. Bricks increasingly

A merchant's house in Stuart London.

19

took the place of plaster between the wooden beams, especially on the Continent, and windows grew larger as the use of glass panes became more common. Houses increased in comfort, but at the same time inroads were made on the open spaces, and buildings began to occupy what had been gardens and orchards. While the structure of houses improved, towns themselves became more crowded as the Middle Ages merged into the Renaissance.

Rising populations and worsening congestion aggravated all the inherited deficiencies of housing and sanitation. Towns in the sixteenth and seventeenth centuries were probably more plague-infested and generally unpleasant than ever they had been during medieval times. The countryside had retreated further from the city centre, but the narrow, sunless alleys, the piles of garbage, the masses of flies, and the open, oozing sewers all remained. Although the houses of successful merchants rose elegantly to four or even five storeys, the homes of ordinary people were poor structures packed closely together to use every inch of space. "As deformed as the minds and confusion of the people," wrote the seventeenth-century London diarist, John Evelyn. Strong words in that faction-torn epoch.

The eighteenth century saw definite advances in building techniques and some attempts to improve sanitary conditions in towns. Brick replaced wood even in England, which had clung persistently to its inflammable half-timbered structures despite the loss of thirteen thousand houses in the Great Fire of London of 1666. A taste for symmetry in architecture had originated in Renaissance Italy, and gradually spread north and west through Europe. As the fashion established itself, it came to affect not only individual houses, but whole streets as well. Cities took on a fresh dignity. In rapidly expanding London, for instance, elegant terraces of houses were built to present symmetrical façades to newly laid-out squares and crescents.

But the improvements were limited to better-class districts. Throughout Europe the drift of people to the cities made life more wretched than ever for the bulk of the population. Accommodation became more expensive and difficult to find, and the poor were crowded into rickety and dilapidated tenements, which sometimes fell about their ears. Dr Samuel Johnson called London, for all its fine new squares, a city whose "falling houses thunder on your head."

Part of the trouble was that many cities were still ringed by their old town walls, although their populations had increased enormously. Outer suburbs encroaching on the countryside did something to relieve congestion, but the amenities and prestige of the traditional centre made many people wish to live in the inner city. Faced with an overcrowding problem, some towns adopted the old Roman solution of building tall apartment blocks for their poorer people instead of allowing them small, individual houses. Edinburgh had high, multi-family dwellings from at least the end of the sixteenth century, but it was the Parisian flats of the eighteenth century which really reintroduced the idea to the world. By 1900 large, specially-designed blocks, that were not mere conversions from big houses fallen on hard times, were a common sight in all the greater cities of Europe and America.

Britain, as the first country to industrialize, experienced housing difficulties of an unprecedented magnitude. Early in the nineteenth century countrymen flocked to work in the factories in ever increasing numbers. Old towns grew alarmingly, and new towns sprang up where only villages had been before. Building could not keep up with demand. Existing houses were divided up into tenements in which only the more fortunate families had a whole room to themselves. Rents were so high and wages so low that people were forced to accept appalling conditions. Some lived in dank, windowless cellars. Others were packed sometimes as many as twenty into a single room. For many the sole accommodation was a rented share in another person's bed. Filth and squalor seemed the inevitable lot of the working man, and drunkenness his only relief. Europe has perhaps never seen such mass degradation as occurred in the growing industrial cities of the early nineteenth century.

Manchester in the 1830s was particularly bad. Smoke belched out by factory chimneys hung like a leaden pall over the city, while blood from the slaughter-houses ran unchecked into the streets to congeal in foul, fly-rimmed puddles. One street of 380 inhabitants had absolutely no sanitary arrangements, so that the people had no choice but to use the public highway as their lavatory.

Most other British cities were little better. It was a story of too many people, and too few houses, drains, and sewers. Some of the three-storey tenements of Glasgow in Scotland, for instance, housed between twelve and twenty persons in every room, but provided them with only the most primitive sanitation. Festering dung heaps mounted inexorably in the tiny courtyards between buildings, threatening the health and offending the nostrils of all the residents. Some profit was, however, gained from the inconvenience. The piles of filth were sold for manure and so helped to pay the rent.

Much of the new housing erected was of a low standard. Many terraces

A Glasgow slum in 1868.

Nineteenth-century industrial housing. Workers' homes were often built back-to-back.

were built back to back, so that the tenants had not even the smallest yard to call their own. Landlords thought only of easy money. If a house stood long enough to make a profit, that was sufficient. Walls were sometimes merely the width of a single brick, while ground floors consisted of compressed earth. Whole rows of houses were known to blow down in a storm.

Britain suffered first, but in time the spread of industrialization created similar conditions in the cities of continental Europe and the United States. American city population trebled in the twenty years from 1820 to 1840, but only at the expense of erecting huge numbers of slum dwellings in Chicago, New York, and other eastern towns. As early as 1834 the squalor of New York tenements excited the indignation of the authors of a sanitary report, but it was 1867 before a city law established minimum standards for all apartment blocks.

In the United States immigration made the housing problem even worse. For the last two decades of the nineteenth century about 400,000 settlers arrived annually, and many went no further than their port of entry, hard-pressed New York. The accommodation shortage became 23

New York slums in 1880.

acute, and unscrupulous landlords were able to charge such high rents that many families could afford only a single room. During the 1890s there were 1,500,000 people crowded into the slum tenements of lower Manhattan.

Asiatic cholera, which sporadically ravaged the overcrowded cities of Europe and America from the 1830s until the last decades of the nineteenth century, gave sanitary reform a great impetus. Slum areas were always nests of contagion, and the risk of infection stirred the middle-class conscience into action. In England, the shocking revelations of the Poor Law Commissioners' reports of 1838 and 1842, coupled with the findings of the Royal Commission on the Health of Towns in 1844 and 1845 convinced many that action was required. Parliament responded with the Shaftesbury Acts of 1851, the first governmental attempt to improve housing conditions. These modest acts gave local authorities the right both to inspect working-class lodging-houses and to commission their construction. Further legislation followed and by 1879 British municipalities were authorized not only to demolish insanitary houses, but also to have new ones built in their place with the help of government loans.

Slum dwellers lived in squalor. The interior of a New York tenement in 1896.

These government measures reinforced the effect of the local bylaws which, following the Public Health Act of 1848, had sought to establish minimum building standards for all future homes. By 1875 no house could be built in a British city unless it had a mains water supply, reasonably high rooms, each with a window, and a backyard at least ten feet square. Low enough standards perhaps, and ones which produced monotonous rows of almost identical houses, but still a great step forward.

Official policies were matched and even preceded by the private efforts of charitable institutions and individuals. In 1844, seven years before the Shaftesbury Acts, a small group of low rental dwellings was built in London by the Society for Improving the Conditions of the Labouring Classes. Two years later another organization formed to help working-class Londoners began to erect a huge, five-storey block of flats. Each of the families lucky enough to be selected was provided with four rooms, piped water and, luxury of luxuries, a lavatory to themselves. London also benefited from the generosity of the American philanthropist George Peabody, who built similar apartment blocks during the 1860s. At last definite attempts, both public and private, were being made to remedy the dreadful conditions created by the rapid expansion of industrial cities.

There was also another side to this grim story of poor housing. Although the nineteenth century reduced the less fortunate to the depths of squalor, it did provide new standards of comfort for the well-to-do. Mains water, flushing lavatories, and proper bathrooms were all innovations which by the end of the century had become established as necessities. House lighting and heating also progressed. Central heating from a water boiler in the cellar was introduced in the United States during the 1830s, while after the formation of the first gas-light company in London in 1812 candles and oil lamps were gradually replaced. Before the century was out gas itself was challenged, and Edison and Swan's electric bulbs furnished a new form of lighting for an increasing minority.

Growing technical expertise held the promise of unparalleled domestic comfort, but only for the rich. Despite government legislation in Britain little was actually done to improve the slum dweller's lot. The laws were permissive. Local authorities had powers to demolish and rebuild, but they were not obliged to use them. In fact until after the First World War only about 5 per cent of the dwellings built each year were commissioned by the municipalities.

The United States was even more wary of governmental intervention. Public action was limited to city or state regulations modelled on the New York tenement house regulations of 1867, which had decreed minimum

A block of flats built in 1868 by the American philanthropist George Peabody to house working families in London.

acceptance standards for sanitation and ventilation. It was not until the troubled Depression era of the 1930s that the Federal Government felt compelled to offer loans for house building programmes.

The prosperous Western countries are still plagued by a residue of unsatisfactory housing. In the United States of 1970 there remain six million substandard dwellings, twenty-two years after the passing of the Urban Renewal Act. Under this and subsequent legislation massive Federal aid has financed the demolition and rebuilding of many run-down urban areas, but especially in the earlier schemes too little thought was given to rehousing the displaced population. Often poorer people found their homes smashed aside to make way for new buildings whose rentals they could no longer afford. Many families have had to move unwillingly into high-rise municipal flats, which although comfortable in themselves can be lonely, and even dangerous, places to live.

Britain and most other European countries are also gripped by chronic housing difficulties, which they seem incapable of completely overcoming. The backlog of poor housing inherited from the past is too great to be swept away overnight. Giant blocks of flats and rows of new houses rise in place of demolished slums, but always there seem yet more aging   27

High-rise flats in Brooklyn, New York City.

Shanty town in Lima, Peru.

buildings to be cleared. In Britain more than two million houses are over one hundred years old.

The housing problems of the Western countries pale into insignificance, however, when compared with those faced by the developing nations. Even the meanest neighbourhoods in modern industrial towns seem fortunate against the unsewered, unwatered, unpaved, and often unlit shanty settlements which huddle around many South American and Asian cities.

The problem of shantytowns erected overnight by squatters has grown to mammoth proportions since the end of the Second World War. Desperate slum dwellers and impoverished peasants descend on an unoccupied suburban district and throw up huts of straw, tin, wood, cardboard, or whatever else comes to hand. Once established, there they stay, defying all the efforts of the police to evict them. The settlements grow and some of the huts are rebuilt in brick, but water still has to be fetched in cans, and sanitation remains unknown. Often the inhabitants are intelligent and responsible, but they cannot prevent their encampments becoming a health and fire risk to the neighbouring city.

Such are the numbers of squatters that rehousing any but a small minority is probably beyond the financial resources of their countries. Peru, with a total population of only twelve million, has nearly a million squatters, half of whom are concentrated about Lima. In Venezuela a third of the inhabitants of Caracas, the capital, are squatters, and in Chile so are a quarter of the people of Santiago. Manila in the Philippines and Ankara in Turkey have problems of similar magnitude.

Even people with more permanent accommodation are often little better off. Three-quarters of the inhabitants of Calcutta, the Indian city which is the world centre of cholera, live in overcrowded tenements. Well over half the families have only one room, and in the very worst slums there is only one water tap to serve thirty and one lavatory to serve twenty people. The world has a long way to go before it can be proud of the way its city dwellers live.

3

City Streets

Modern brightly lit streets, filled with traffic for most hours of the day, are the product of the slow development which began over five thousand years ago with the narrow alleys of the early Sumerian cities. Throughout this time wheeled vehicles have been known, but not until the nineteenth century did passenger travel about town become either available or really essential to the ordinary man. In the much smaller cities of earlier days most people walked, and streets were intended mainly for pedestrian use.

Most streets in the towns of ancient Sumeria were too narrow for any wheeled traffic at all. Houses whose blank, windowless walls reflected the harsh sunlight flanked the unpaved alleys so closely that little room was left even for pedestrians. However, archaeologists know that occasional donkey riders thrust their way through the protesting crowds, because mounting blocks have been unearthed alongside some of the ancient, ruined houses.

Although the streets of Sumerian towns were little more than irregular spaces left between dwellings, later inhabitants of Mesopotamia did produce one of the most impressive ceremonial roads of all time. Nebuchadnezzar, who reigned from 605 to 562 B.C., determined to make the city of Babylon into a worthy capital for his vast empire. As part of this programme he constructed a great processional way stretching from the suburbs through the Ishtar Gate (dedicated to the goddess of love) into the inner walled city with its famous ziggurat and temples. The alluvial land of Mesopotamia was without surface rock, but white limestone and red breccia were brought in from abroad to pave the entire length of the sixty-three-feet-wide highway. Outside the Ishtar Gate, the road was flanked on either side by high walls, faced with glazed blue bricks and decorated at intervals with almost life-size lions in raised relief. The gate itself was also covered in gleaming blue brick, but its embellishment consisted of alternate rows of red and white bulls and dragons.

In striking contrast to this single majestic avenue, most of Babylon's

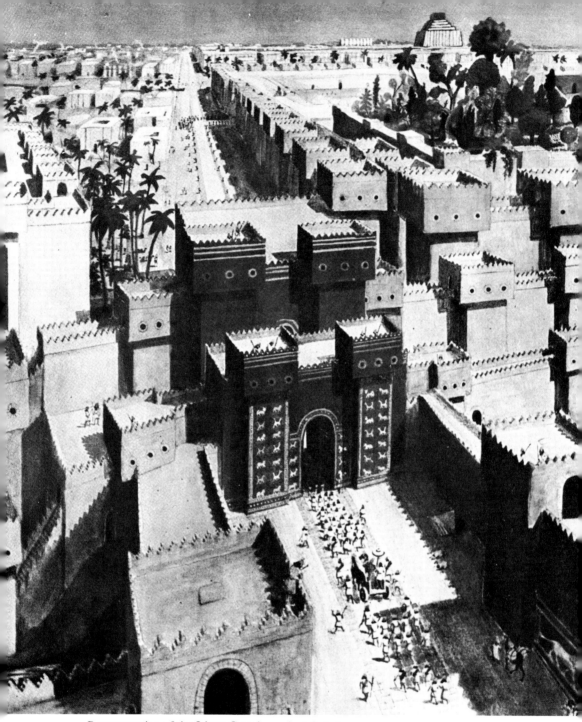

Reconstruction of the Ishtar Gate in ancient Babylon.

streets were narrow and dirty, while all were normally left completely unlit after dark. City life halted at nightfall except during religious festivals, so it was only on these occasions that Babylon needed to roll out the hundredweight jars of fat, whose thick, slow burning wicks provided a feeble light for its streets.

As far as is known, Egyptian and Indus townsmen fared no better than their Mesopotamian contemporaries for either transport or street lighting. Wagons there were in plenty, in fact clay models of bullock carts are common finds in the Indus cities, but these vehicles were used to carry goods rather than passengers. City streets remained very much the preserve of pedestrians.

In Greek times some town houses had stables, but since most streets were narrow, horse traffic could never have been heavy. Anyway, Greek towns were generally so compact that all important buildings were within easy walking distance for every citizen. There was little need for transport except for prestige purposes.

Rome was the greatest city of the ancient world, and the first to run into serious trouble with traffic congestion. Unplanned and unchecked growth had left it with a chaotic street system. Its broadest roads were only twenty-one feet wide and the majority measured from sixteen down to a mere nine feet across. The press of pedestrians competing with goods wagons and horsemen in these narrow lanes caused such confusion and delay that the dictator, Julius Caesar, felt compelled to take action. His solution to the problem was typically thorough and ruthless. All wheeled vehicles, except ceremonial chariots and builders' wagons, were banished from the streets during daylight hours. Market carts had to wait until dusk before rumbling into town.

Caesar's regulations remained in force after his death, and kept the streets of Rome almost free of heavy vehicles in daytime, though not without creating another problem. The noise of swearing teamsters, straining horses, and groaning axles kept half the city awake at night. According to the satirist Juvenal, who lived from about A.D 60 to 140, even the Emperor found it difficult to sleep. This, however, did not prevent a stoical Emperor of later times, Marcus Aurelius, from extending the ban on daylight traffic to every city in the Roman Empire.

Strangely enough for a city which insisted that provisions for its markets should be brought in after sunset, Rome had absolutely no street lighting. On moonless nights, when the metropolis was plunged into darkness, the only lights in the streets were the flaring torches of revellers brave enough to venture out or the brands carried by armed slaves escorting a wealthy   33

A model showing the chaotic street system of central Rome about A.D. 300.

master to a party. Danger lurked in every gloomy alley. Around each corner might wait a gang of murderous delinquents. Juvenal's quip, that only a fool would go out to supper without making a will, was too near the truth for comfort. Nearly everyone went home as soon as it got dark, and locked themselves and their property securely inside.

The cities of the Eastern Roman Empire were more advanced in the matter of lighting than the old Western capital on the Tiber. Fourth-century Antioch, then a city of a quarter million inhabitants, certainly had some form of illumination since one of its natives, Libanius, who lived from A.D. 314 to 393, wrote of a party of drunks slashing with their swords at the ropes which supported the street lamps. Taxes levied for street lighting are mentioned in the famous law code of the Emperor Justinian, A.D. 483 to 565, so it seems probable that all major Byzantine cities were lit at night.

About the time that Roman power was decaying in Europe, Central America was experiencing an upsurge of urbanization. Great cities like Teotihuacán in Mexico grew and flourished without the aid of a single wheeled vehicle, since carts were unknown in pre-Columbian America. In

Mayan and also in the later Aztec cities ordinary people walked everywhere. The only form of passenger transport was the litter, and this was reserved for chiefs.

Medieval Europe did not lack the wheel, but none of its towns was big enough to need passenger transport. Humble citizens could easily walk from one part of their city to another, and nobles rode in town more for dignity than from necessity. However, the movement of goods did require vehicles of a sort. Sledges and barrows, pushed or pulled by men, were widely used to shift light merchandise and building materials, but those streets which were wide enough also carried heavy wheeled traffic. Food, firewood, and casks of wine were all carried into town on horse-drawn carts.

Long before the era of mass transport, the cities of the Middle Ages had their own traffic problems to overcome. Streets were so narrow that progress was slow at the best of times, but to make things worse citizens were not above surreptitiously extending their property to encroach on what little road there was. During the fourteenth century one man even went so far as to build a cook-shop across the high street of Wells, a town in western England. Perhaps the food he sold was particularly good, for seven years went by before his fellow townsmen forced him to pull down the obstruction. Other offenders were less blatant, and were usually dealt with quickly. Most municipal authorities were vigilant in their defence of the public right-of-way. Even the king could not get away with obstructing his own highways. In 1312 the aldermen of London politely requested King Edward II to reconsider a building scheme which would have narrowed a road used by firewood carts coming up from the river.

Some towns, of which fourteenth-century Bristol was one, insisted on an early form of "off street parking." Market people had to stable their horses rather than leave them standing to block the road. Other cities had regulations aimed at safety. The city government of London issued a stern warning in the fourteenth century against speeding in empty carts, while several towns ordered that horses and cattle should be carefully controlled on their way to watering places, because of the danger to pedestrians from runaway beasts.

Then there was the problem of the pigs. Nearly all medieval townsmen kept some, and nobody objected as long as the animals were confined to private gardens and supervised during their daily journeys to and from the common grazing land outside the city walls. Trouble came only when those too idle to care for their pigs properly turned them loose to forage in the streets. Things once got to such a state in London that during the 35 reign of King Edward I orders were given to kill any stray pig on sight. But the medieval hog was irrepressible. Monarchs came and went, but the pig survived to plague city streets well into Tudor times. The pig-keeping habit even crossed the Atlantic. At the beginning of the nineteenth century the streets of New York were still infested with free-roaming swine.

During the earlier Middle Ages city streets were deserted as soon as night fell. Curfew regulations kept people indoors from dusk to sunrise, so that street lighting was not required. In later times citizens were allowed to stay out after dark to celebrate great religious feasts like Christmas, and on these occasions many householders hung up lamps to light the way. This was the beginning of street lighting in European towns. Gradually it became not only the custom but the law that each family should light the front of its home. London's aldermen were ordered to see that every house hung out its lantern for the Christmas feast of the year 1405, and by 1415 wealthier Londoners were required to keep a lamp burning on all moonless winter nights. The citizens of Paris were also expected to take responsibility for lighting their streets. On orders issued by King Louis XI in 1461 every house in the French capital was to display a light in a window. However, even if they had been fully obeyed these measures would have given only feeble illumination, and it was all too easy to claim that the wind had snuffed out a candle.

A seventeenth-century etching of a hackney coach driving through the piazza in London's Covent Garden.

A sedan chair from a drawing made in 1655.

While the townsmen of Medieval Europe trudged their gloomy, pig-befouled alleys the more civilized Chinese were disporting themselves in fine carriages. The Venetian traveller, Marco Polo (*c.* 1254 to 1324) who visited India and China during the thirteenth century has left a fascinating account of life in Kinsai, modern Hangchow. In this great and prosperous city, with its well-paved streets, numerous pleasure-coaches were hired out after work had finished for the day. Wives and girlfriends were carried around town in high style, reclining on cushions beneath gay coloured awnings. European cities were to see no comparable carriage-parades before five more centuries had elapsed.

It was not until the seventeenth century that vehicles began to ply for hire on the streets of European cities, and even then only the rich could afford the fares. Hackney coaches probably began to operate in London as early as 1625, and certainly by 1634 there was the equivalent of a modern taxi rank in the Strand. Another sort of conveyance, the sedan chair, which became increasingly popular as the century progressed, was first introduced into England from the Continent in 1634. The solitary passenger entered through a door at the front, and sat in splendour viewing the world through glass-paned windows as two burly porters carried him to his destination.

Streets remained filthy and deeply rutted during the seventeenth 37 century, but more care was taken to illuminate them at night. After 1667 Paris was lit on moonless evenings by lanterns paid for out of the public taxes. By the end of the century the French capital had about sixty-five hundred lanterns, each provided with a candle big enough to burn until past midnight. Candles were issued to so called "lanterniers," who during their enforced year of office had to respond every night to the call of a hand bell summoning them out to light their appointed fifteen lanterns.

London moved towards publicly maintained lighting in 1657 when it decided to provide lamps in various important places which were too far from inhabited houses to be adequately lit. More efficient lamps also appeared during the last part of the century and oil began to displace candles. In 1694 the city of London allowed Edward Hemming to install an oil lamp outside every tenth house and to charge all the householders in the street a yearly lighting fee of six shillings. Anyone who opted out of this scheme had to hang out a lantern according to the old regulations. Eventually in 1736 London did away with intermediary contractors and took over direct responsibility for its own lighting. An annual lighting rate was charged, but the five thousand oil lamps which were provided made London the best lit city of that time and a model for all other towns to follow.

Besides these advances in lighting the seventeenth century also witnessed the first attempt to give the public at large a means of getting about town. The French writer Blaise Pascal, shortly before his death in 1662, financed a number of coaches which followed fixed routes in Paris, picking up passengers along the way. Pascal had intended the services to be open to everybody, but the French government would not allow ordinary people to ride in case they developed ideas above their stations in life. The enterprise floundered through lack of custom and probably did not long survive its author's death.

Despite Pascal's efforts, urban transport for the masses did not become a reality until the nineteenth century. Several forms of vehicle were eventually developed, but first on the scene was the omnibus. During the early years of the century such large cities as London and Paris already had short-haul stagecoaches to carry passengers into town from the suburbs. These vehicles were, however, conventional in their design and ill adapted to the needs of a short journey. One French visitor to London complained bitterly after a two-hour trip in such a coach in 1810. The getting up and down of passengers, the tearing of women's petticoats, the swearing and the delay called forth his exasperated comment: "I never saw anything so ill managed." To add insult to injury the fares were exorbitantly high.

An improved vehicle was finally invented by another Frenchman, Stanislas Baudry, who entered the transport business more by accident than design. In 1823 he was the owner of a bath-house in the suburbs of Nantes, and to oblige his customers he ran a coach from the town centre out to his establishment. Before long Baudry found that many of his passengers had no intention of bathing, but simply wanted transport to the outskirts of the city. This gave him the idea of starting regular suburban services with vehicles designed to allow passengers to get on and off without treading too much on one another's toes. Baudry's original coach had started its journey from outside the shop of a M. Omnes, whose motto "Omnes omnibus"—"Omnes for everyone"—is generally supposed to have resulted in the name "omnibus" being coined for the new conveyance.

Early in 1828 Baudry moved his sphere of operations to Paris, where he was given permission to work ten routes. Omnibuses proved an instant

London's first bus service was started by George Shillibeer in 1829.

success in the capital, and within a few months of their introduction each coach was carrying over three hundred passengers a day. Competitors appeared and omnibuses were built with feverish haste.

One of those who profited from this sudden demand for new vehicles was George Shillibeer, an English coachbuilder with connections in Paris. Shillibeer quickly saw that omnibuses would have a future in other cities, but his initial move to start similar services in London was thwarted by the British Treasury, which had given hackney carriage owners exclusive rights in the central regions of the town. However, Shillibeer was not to be deterred, and in 1829 he established London's first bus route just outside the preserve of the hackney carriages. His vehicles were very large by the standards of their day. Each could seat twenty passengers and needed three horses to pull it.

A streetcar which ran on the world's first city tramway laid down by John Stephenson in New York, 1832.

It is not certain who introduced the omnibus to America, but possibly Abraham Bower can claim the honour. He inaugurated a service in New York in 1830, and it was in this same bustling, expanding city that an entirely new type of urban transport was devised a few years later. Many streets in the fast-growing towns of the United States were at this time inadequately paved, so that a ride in a conventional road-vehicle was often a bone-shaking experience. The state of the roads and the then current craze for railways led a young Irish immigrant, John Stephenson, to create the horse-drawn streetcar, which rolled smoothly over rails laid through the city thoroughfares. A track was constructed between the Bowery and Fourteenth Street in New York, and in 1832 Stephenson and two fellow-countrymen opened the world's first public tram service.

Streetcars did not catch on as quickly as omnibuses, for although their smooth track enabled the horses to haul a heavier load of passengers the initial cost and the maintenance of the permanent way was an intimidating financial burden. New Orleans opened a four mile long tramway in 1835, but it was not until the 1850s and '60s that the use of the streetcar really began to spread. Paris experimented with a service in 1853, and other European cities such as Berlin, Brussels, Copenhagen, and Vienna followed suit during the 1860s. London had tried trams briefly in 1861, but had not liked them. Some ten years had to elapse before the streetcar was accepted by the British capital.

Just as characteristic of the mid-nineteenth century as the horse-buses and trams were the gas lamps which lit the city streets. The major figure in the early development of gas was the Scottish engineer William Murdoch, who in 1792 began to burn vapour distilled from coal to light his office at Redruth, Cornwall. Ten years later during the celebrations which marked a truce in the Napoleonic Wars, Murdoch was able to make sufficient gas to contribute to a special illumination of his employers' factory, the famous Boulton and Watt engineering works at Birmingham. This factory was later the site of the world's first gasholder.

Every new idea needs a publicist. German-born Frederick Albert Winser was the self-appointed champion of gas. In 1803 Winser came to England for a campaign of lectures and demonstrations on the benefits of gas lighting. In 1807 he got permission to light fashionable Pall Mall. People flocked to see the thirteen hollow iron lamp posts each with three glass globes in which the gas flames flickered. Many shook their heads in suspicion and disbelief, and Sir Walter Scott, the novelist, wrote scathingly to a friend of "a madman proposing to light London with — what do you think? Why, with smoke!" But the sceptics were wrong. The Gas Light and Coke Company was formed in 1812 and by 1823 over 215 miles of London's streets were lit by gas.

As the nineteenth century progressed many attempts were made to find a replacement for the horse as the streetcar's motive power. John Stephenson had experimented unsuccessfully with steam traction on the original tramway in New York, and by 1860 techniques had improved sufficiently for Philadelphia to keep six steam-powered trams in everyday use. Another idea was to hitch streetcars to a cable running beneath the road, so that 41

42

Cartoon showing public reaction to Winser's demonstration of gas street-lighting, 1807–1808.

they could be winched along from a central motor-house. Cable tramways enjoyed a considerable vogue in the United States after 1873 when San Francisco had shown they would work even on its hilly streets. Along with the workable systems, there were some very strange experiments. Naphtha, compressed air, ammonia, and even clockwork motors were all tried before Siemens' patient work in Germany led to a feasible electric tram.

The first public electric tramway, opened in a Berlin suburb in 1881, was only one-and-a-half miles long, but such were the advantages of electricity that within twenty years there were fifteen thousand miles of electrified track in the United States alone. During the first quarter of the twentieth century electric trams were the principal form of urban transport in most large cities, but as motor traffic increased the importance of the streetcar slowly waned. In America, the home of the streetcar, only a few cities retained their tracks, and in Britain, too, trams have all but disappeared. On the Continent of Europe, however, many cities still have extensive networks, and a number of German towns have ambitious plans to operate trams in subways to relieve surface traffic. Further east, Russia and the Asian countries still employ trams in many cities. Moscow, Karachi, Calcutta all still know the distinctive clank and rattle of the streetcar.

The high cost of track installation and the general improvement in the surfacing of city streets led to the development of the trolleybus, which drew electricity from overhead wires but ran free like a motorcoach. Siemens experimented with trolleybuses before 1900, and during the succeeding decade several other inventors attempted to perfect vehicles of the same type. Leeds and Bradford, which adopted trolleybuses in 1911, were the first British towns to use what were then called "trackless trams."

A two-coach trolleybus in Moscow.

Electric Jablochkoff candles used to light the Avenue de l'Opéra in Paris, 1878.

Trolleybuses were quiet, gave out no fumes, had good acceleration and, unlike trams, could pull into the curb so that other road traffic was not completely halted while passengers got on and off. Gradually the trolleybus found favour, and during the late 1920s and the 1930s several large tram operators began to convert to the more flexible conveyance. Trolleybuses still run in several major cities. Moscow for instance has some articulated two-coach vehicles which can cram in two hundred passengers in the rush hour, but the tendency seems to be for "trackless" as well as "tracked" trams to be replaced by motor buses.

The development of efficient generators in the 1870s provided a new form of power for city lighting. Mains electricity was first used to light a 45

London's last horse-bus over Waterloo Bridge ran in 1913.

city street in the French capital, Paris, where during 1878 sixty-two Jablochkoff candles, a sort of arc lamp named after their inventor, the Russian Paul Jablochkoff, were installed along the Avenue de l'Opéra. A year later lamps of the same kind were used to illuminate a one-and-a-quarter-mile stretch of road in London, while Cleveland, Ohio, became the first United States town to try electric light, when it erected twelve American Brush type arc lamps in one of its squares.

Electric lighting was taken up by other cities, particularly at first in the

United States. But although the original arc lamps were a great improvement on gas as far as light output was concerned, they were expensive to run and burnt away quickly. An alternative device was clearly needed. Two inventors, the American, Edison, and the Englishman, Swan, initially working in opposition before joining forces, perfected an incandescent filament bulb with a much more acceptable life span. Swan gave the first large scale demonstration of street lighting with the new type of lamp at Newcastle, England, in 1881, but arcs continued in use for many years because of the brilliant light they shed. Since the 1930s filament lamps have themselves been increasingly displaced, and today's cities are mainly lit by the garish light of gaseous discharge lamps.

Returning to street transport, motor buses were the natural consequence of Benz and Daimler's successful development of the automobile during the 1880s. Strangely enough, horse-drawn buses were not quickly superseded, and, despite a few experiments with internal combustion engines, the only mechanically driven public vehicles on the streets at the beginning of the present century were trams. Within a decade, however, the picture had completely changed. London's motor-bus fleet, for instance, grew from a mere twenty in number at the beginning of 1905 to well over a thousand by mid-1908. Similar advances occurred in the other great cities of the world, as the draught-horse swiftly approached the end of its long career. Gradually the motor bus proved its superiority to electric trams and trolleybuses, taking over from them in town after town, until now it is the predominant form of surface public transport in most cities of the world.

Trains also play an important part in urban transport. They were the first successful form of mechanical vehicle and, since the opening of the earliest public line in 1825, have done much to encourage city growth by providing rapid transit from the outskirts so the centre.

City railways are costly to construct because they take up valuable building land. As early as the 1830s the engineer Robert Stephenson evolved a scheme for running trains through tunnels under London to avoid expensive demolitions, but thirty years were to pass before other railway men translated his idea into reality. The world's first underground railway, London's three-and-three-quarter-mile-long Metropolitan line, was opened to the public in January 1863. Despite the discomfort caused to the passengers by fumes from the steam locomotives, the little railway was an immediate and lasting success. In the first year of operations alone over nine million people were carried, and thereafter passengers and revenue actually increased. Later extensions were not always so popular. The Times of London of 7 October 1884 described a journey on the newly   47

A station on London's Metropolitan railway, the world's first underground which was opened in 1863.

opened Inner Circle line as "a form of mild torture" and complained of the "sulphurous fumes" belched out by the steam locomotives.

In December 1890 the City and South London Railway opened the first subway to use electric locomotives, so overcoming once and for all the problem of poisonous fumes left hanging in the tunnels. There were breakdowns and technical difficulties, and the carriages with their tiny, high-up windows were jokingly called "padded cells," but this pioneer line convinced many other cities that underground trains were both possible and desirable. Budapest opened a two-and-a-half-mile-long electrically operated subway in 1896, Paris began to build its famous Metro in 1898, while the Berlin U-bahn got under way in 1902. New York was a little slower because of its previous reliance on elevated railroads, but by 1904 it had opened a short stretch of what was to grow into the world's largest purely underground system with 240 miles of tunnels. Nowadays over thirty of the world's great cities, ranging from Tokyo in Japan to Buenos Aires in Argentina and from Montreal in Canada to Moscow in Russia, use underground trains to combat congestion in surface traffic.

48   Even in the days of horse-drawn vehicles, overcrowding in the streets

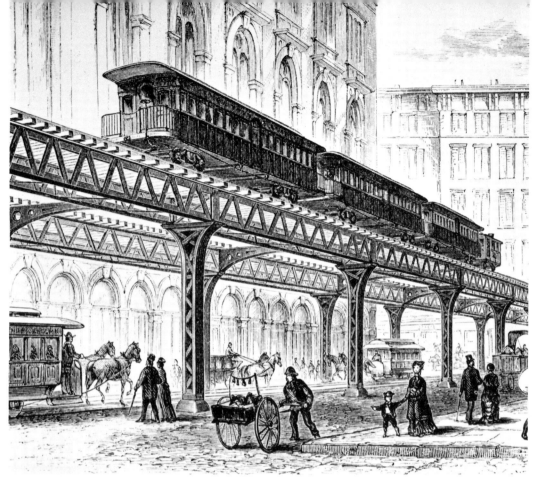

New York's elevated railway in Third Avenue in the 1880's.

was a serious problem, and since the advent of the motorcar the situation has worsened dramatically. Exhaust fumes, the noise of revving engines, and the difficulty of crossing the road make life unpleasant for people on foot, while the slow crawl of the traffic and the scarcity of parking spaces infuriate the drivers.

The cities of America have been the first to adapt themselves to the needs of the automobile era. Expressways, built at enormous cost, speed transit into the city centre, and off-street parking on a massive scale helps to keep the streets uncluttered. Planners are not entirely satisfied with the results. Road improvements are promptly swamped by traffic increases, car parks gobble up valuable building sites, and automobiles pour into town in even greater numbers.

In the United States many municipalities plan to coax commuters away from their cars by improving public transport. Washington and San Francisco intend building entirely new subways, while New York and Chicago are considering extensions to their existing networks. London   49

Cleveland, U.S.A., has constructed multi-laned highways to speed traffic flow.

The StaRRcar, a possible form of automated transport for the future.

has already set an example by adding the new Victoria Line to its tube system. San Francisco's tunnels form a link in a vast electric rail complex partly opened in 1969 but planned to serve the whole Bay Area in the 1970s. Fast electric trains will average 40 mph and touch double that speed, but a sophisticated signalling system will permit rush hour services to run at only ninety-second intervals.

Besides these conventional projects, more futuristic possibilities have been mooted or even employed. Chicago has already toyed with the idea of automatic buses responding to control impulses from a cable running under the road surface. On such an automated road, vehicles would be able to travel close together at high speed without danger of collision, so that a greater density of traffic could be carried than on an ordinary highway. An American inventor, William Alden, is responsible for a more flexible and personal mode of transport. His "StaRRcars" — the name comes from "self transit rail and road" — are small electric automobiles which commuters may one day drive through suburban streets to local pickup points of a special ramp leading into the city centre. Once the StaRRcar is on the track, automatic control will take over and, having pressed a button to select his exit point, the passenger will be able to sit back and relax.

Possibly more immediately practicable is the idea of a pool of self-drive electric minicars for use in central areas. Drivers would leave their conventional automobiles in carparks on the outskirts and continue their 51 journeys in much smaller, silent, and fume-free electric runabouts. In 1959 a scheme for a fleet of free, publicly financed vehicles got as far as serious consideration in Paris, but was finally abandoned. It is more usually suggested that cars should be worked on the coin in the slot principle.

Moving pavements are another possible way of lessening the need for private vehicles. The idea itself is by no means new. As long ago as 1874 a moving pavement was suggested for New York, but never adopted because of cost and technical difficulties. One obvious shortcoming of the original design was that no provision was made for passengers to board or alight from the travelling belt. If any worthwhile speed had been achieved people would have been hurled to the ground when they tried to step off. This particular problem was solved in 1888 by Rettig's concept of three parallel tracks running at different speeds. Passengers were to board a slow moving surface, to transfer to the middle track, and then step onto the fast pavement. They were to return to the slow lane only when nearing

A moving pavement proposed for New York in 1874.

their destination. A modification of this scheme using just two tracks was employed with great success in the world's first moving pavement, which was built in Chicago for the Columbian Exposition of 1893.

Similar pavements were subsequently shown at the Berlin exhibition of 1896 and at the Paris exhibition of 1900. The Paris pavement was particularly popular, and during the eight months for which it was open to the public it carried over six million people with no serious mishap. Some twenty years later moving pavements were again in the news in Paris, when its city government pondered the merits of a system of passenger conveyor belts working through tunnels. About the same time New York had an almost identical plan for an underground moving pavement to run between Times Square and Grand Central Station. Both schemes came to nothing.

At the present time the use of moving pavements seems to be limited to airports and railway stations where a steady stream of passengers can be guaranteed. The Bank Underground Station in London has a three-hundred-foot "travolator," while the Châtelet Station in Paris has an even longer passenger conveyor. Los Angeles Airport in the United States also possesses a moving pavement. All these systems have single speed tracks which passengers board in the same way as escalators. Speeds are therefore slow, something in the region of $2\frac{1}{2}$ mph, so that this kind of conveyor is suitable only for short journeys.

Rather similar to the moving pavement is the "carveyor," which features a continuous line of small cabins carried along on a rubber belt. Between stations the cabins spread out and are whisked along at 15 mph, but at the pickup points they bunch together as the belt slows down to $1\frac{1}{2}$ mph to match the speed of a moving platform. Several American cities, including Los Angeles and Atlanta, have studied the idea, but at the moment no public carveyor is in existence in a town, though the "car-lator" used by skiers at the Lake Biwa resort in Japan embodies the same concept.

For fast transit between the city centre and important destinations like the local airport, monorails have much to offer. They can be built more cheaply than undergrounds, while if slung above existing roads they need require little or no demolition of property. Tokyo already has a monorail link to its airport, and there seems little doubt that in time many other cities will follow suit. Monorails are, however, by no means new. Wuppertal in Germany still uses one built in 1901. Monorail development has hung fire for so many years mainly because of the ugly raised track and the noise of operations — the very reasons for the removal of elevated railroads from American cities. Modern architecture and technology have 53

Photomontage of France's "Urba Train", an advanced form of monorail.

largely removed both objections, so that monorails should enjoy an increasing popularity. One recent and ingenious design to come out of France is the "Urba Train" which features suction suspension from an overhead track and silent linear electric motor propulsion. An experimental line at Lyon should be operative in 1972.

Many novel and improved modes of transport are available for cities of the future. Monorails, carveyors, moving pavements, electric cars, and automated buses may all have a part to play. Private automobiles will continue to be important, but it is to be hoped that better public transport will prevent them usurping the city environment as they have already begun to do in many industrial nations. If technology is used sensibly, travel in city streets can be made easier and safer, and the whole tone of city life improved.

4

Food and Drink

As soon as people cut themselves off from immediate contact with the land by building cities, they faced the problem of transporting food from the surrounding countryside into their settlements. While towns remained small sufficient food could be brought in easily enough on the backs of men or animals, but ships, roads and carts, and a sophisticated political system were needed to bring the agricultural produce of a wider region within the grasp of an expanding city. A city could not outgrow the ability of its citizens to supply themselves with food.

In early Mesopotamia much of the land was temple property, and the farmers, as tenants of the gods, were expected to hand in a proportion of their produce to the city priests. Barley grain, cheese, dates, and vegetables all poured into the temple storehouses together with the fish that

Food for the Indus cities must have been carried in carts similar to this model found at Mohenjo-daro.

were caught in great numbers in the rivers and irrigation dykes. Meso-potamian cities were small, probably none exceeding twenty thousand inhabitants, and irrigation agriculture provided more than enough food for everyone. Stocks were kept in the temple granaries against disastrous floods or bad harvests, but by the middle of the third millennium B.C. barley was so plentiful in normal years that a surplus could be exported to the mountainous regions of what is now Iran in exchange for the blue, semi-precious stone, lapis lazuli, much coveted by the Sumerians.

In ancient Egypt too, the authorities exercised a careful control over the food supply. The Bible tells how Joseph advised the Pharaoh to compel his subjects to "lay up corn under the hand of Pharaoh, and let them keep food in the cities."

As with the Egyptian towns, each city of the Indus Valley possessed a communal storehouse to receive the agricultural surplus of the surrounding countryside. The main crops have been identified as wheat and barley from actual grains discovered at many sites, but occasional traces of such things as dates and peas show that other plants were cultivated. After harvesting, transport into the cities was almost certainly provided by bullock carts of which numerous terracotta models have been unearthed. At Mohenjo-daro the granary stood on the very edge of the citadel plat-form above what seems to have been an unloading bay for carts. The Indus people kept animals for slaughter as well as for draught purposes. Skeletal remains of sheep and goats have been found together with cattle bones so chopped and splintered that they have obviously passed through the hands of butcher and cook. Far from venerating cows, as do modern Hindus, the Indus city dwellers ate them.

The Greek cities were the first to outgrow the food resources of their immediate environment. Shortages at home forced the Greeks to look outwards. Some towns began to specialize in overseas trade, and from the eighth century B.C. colonies were founded around the Mediterranean, both to relieve local overpopulation and to serve as mercantile outposts abroad. Food imports were paid for partly by the carrying services of Greek shipping, but also by exporting manufactured goods like the famous woollens of Corinth or such agricultural specialities as the oil and wines of Athens.

Commerce and trade made Athens, for a time, the most powerful Greek city, but its dependence on transport made it vulnerable. The whole city-state contained only 120 square miles of agricultural land to feed a total urban and country population of about seventy thousand people.

By the time of the Peloponnesian War, which was fought against Sparta

Painting on a fifth-century B.C. vase showing the type of merchant-ship which brought food supplies to Athens.

between 431 and 404 B.C., Athens was so reliant on corn imported from the Black Sea coast of what is now the U.S.S.R. that it was eventually starved into surrender when blockading enemy warships closed its trade routes in 405 B.C.

Rome increased its available food supply by conquest and efficient transport to such an extent that its population was able to rise to perhaps a million people. Grain poured into the hungry capital from North Africa, Egypt, and as far away as the Black Sea provinces. Given a fair wind, a large grain ship carrying 250 tons of wheat could reach the mouth of the Tiber from Alexandria in eleven days, but the cargo had then to be transferred to smaller vessels for the final journey up river to Rome.

Something like a third of the inhabitants of Rome benefited by a free issue of corn from the immense stocks kept in the imperial granaries. In the time of the Emperor Augustus 150,000 male citizens are said to have collected a monthly corn dole on behalf of their families. One Roman wrote mockingly that the mob thought of nothing but free bread and circuses.

Before the seat of Roman power was transferred to Constantinople arrangements were made for Egypt to supply the new capital with grain. Wheat imports were always carefully controlled by the government, and the price of bread was fixed. The Roman custom of providing the poor

Second-century A. D. Roman mosaic showing the distribution of the corn dole.

with a food hole was continued. State bakeries supplied free bread, although after the loss of the traditional corn producing area with the fall of Egypt to the Arabs in A.D. 642, the number of recipients of the dole had to be cut back.

In the Eastern Empire Constantinople struggled to keep food prices stable. The Imperial government also imposed all sorts of restrictions in its efforts to ensure that the populace was properly fed in times of emergency. Local farmers were not allowed to slaughter their cows for sale to city butchers, in case a sudden invasion found the vicinity of the town temporarily destitute of cattle. Another rule instructed householders to store enough food to last out a three-year siege.

Most of the towns which grew up during the earlier medieval period in what had been the western provinces of the Roman Empire were so small that their food requirements could be easily met by local agriculture. The general size of towns may be judged from the fact that London, with a population of only some 50,000 as late as 1400, was by far the largest city in England. However, on the Continent a few much larger towns had developed during the fourteenth century. Florence had 100,000 citizens about the middle of the century, while Paris had perhaps as many as a quarter of a million. These giant cities imported food from a distance, but the vast majority of ordinary towns served as market outlets for very limited areas.

So matters stood until the Industrial Revolution at the close of the eighteenth century ushered in the age of super-cities. In 1800 London was the only city in the world with more than a million people; by the 1960s eighty cities were to have populations exceeding this figure.

Such unprecedented growth would have been impossible but for improvements in agriculture, the opening up of new farming lands, and startling advances in transport and technology. Farming methods have grown steadily better ever since the eighteenth century. Crop rotation, fertilization, the development of new strains of cereals, and the selective breeding of livestock have all contributed to a greatly increased yield, while at the same time mechanization has diminished the need for farm labour.

As industrialization spread in the European homelands, pioneers thrust their way into new territories. Untamed land in western America, Australasia, and southern Africa was subjected to the plough or felt the tread of the hooves of grazing cattle. A greater area than ever before was brought under cultivation.

The world's new resources of food production would have been of no value, however, if the means had not been at hand to link remote rural areas to the great centres of population. Without the railways and steamships, which were developed during the nineteenth century, the modern, town-dominated world could never have come into being.

It took some time for the full impact of advances in transport to make itself felt. Until about 1870 most of the food for Europe's industrial towns was locally grown, but after this date steamships and railways, aided by developments in canning and refrigeration, enabled a vast growth of international trade in perishable foods. Canned beef from Argentina was first shipped to Britain in the 1860s, while the earliest consignment of refrigerated Australian meat arrived in London in 1880 aboard the SS *Strathleven*. The agricultural wealth of the western states of America was also made more accessible as railways were driven across the continent after the Civil War. Cheaper meat and grain flooded into the eastern states and across the Atlantic to Europe. Industrial cities could now draw on the whole world for the extra food they needed for their growth.

Early townsmen had to transport food some distance into their cities, 59 but they ensured that nature delivered their water. Most ancient towns were built on the banks of a river or at the very least where a copious spring bubbled to the surface. Water could be had simply by a short walk to the riverside. As cities grew bigger and the walk longer, the labour of carrying heavy pitchers up from the water's edge persuaded some citizens to dig wells closer to their homes. Rising populations also inevitably caused an increase in river pollution, so that water-borne diseases became a serious problem. Cities learned to stretch out aqueducts to tap purer, more distant sources, but not until the nineteenth century did they discover methods for treating contaminated water and making it fit to drink.

In the arid land of Mesopotamia urban life was unthinkable away from the rivers, which provided both drinking water for the citizens and irrigation for their fields. Drawing water from the river must have been a daily chore for most Mesopotamian households, though a few thought it worth their while to gain a private, unpolluted supply by digging themselves a well. The realization that water can usually be found by delving into the earth is very old. A well discovered at the city of Eshnunna, about twenty-five miles northeast of modern Baghdad, is thought to date back to the third millennium B.C.

Before any cities developed in Egypt, farmers had been able to collect enough rainwater in specially dug tanks to last them through the dry

A typical brick-lined well in Mohenjo-daro.

season. Gradually, however, the climate grew drier, and rainfall became so infrequent that most of the cultivators were forced to migrate to within reach of the River Nile, their only reliable source of water. The river became a highway, linking the previously isolated farming villages together and facilitating the spread of ideas and the exchange of knowledge. Civilization in Egypt was the gift of the Nile.

Ordinary Egyptian city dwellers relied on the river or the irrigation ditches for all their water needs. The Bible tells of the distress caused when the Nile once became so polluted that millions of fish floated dead to the surface, leaving the desperate Egyptians to dig frantically "round about the river for water to drink; for they could not drink of the water of the river."

Indus Valley townsmen preferred to dig wells rather than carry water from the rivers. At Mohenjo-daro, for example, most housing blocks had one or two wells, neatly lined with burnt mud brick. In addition to these private sources there were public wells open to all.

The cities of sixth-century B.C. Greece also regarded it as a civic responsibility to organize an adequate supply of water for everybody. Athenian laws of that time guaranteed the use of a public well to any citizen without one of his own, and strictly forbade the pollution of springs by the washing of clothing:

Most Greek towns relied on springs and wells within their own walls, because dependence on external sources would have made them vulnerable in war. Some cities, however, outgrew their original supplies and were forced to look for water outside their defences. Aqueducts, to bring water from a distance, were not a Greek invention. Their origin is, in fact, uncertain, but they were undoubtedly used in Mesopotamia many years before the Greeks thought of them. The remains of a nine-hundred-yard-long causeway, built by the seventh-century B.C. Assyrian king Sennacherib to carry irrigation water over a valley, still exist. The Greek achievement was rather to be the first to supply drinking water for ordinary citizens by means of aqueducts.

Greek aqueducts usually consisted of terracotta pipes hidden underground out of sight of marauding enemy soldiers. One of the earliest, dating from the sixth century B.C., supplied the city of Vathy on the island of Samos. Earthenware pipes led water from a spring to a mile-long tunnel hacked through the solid rock of an intervening hill. At the other end of the tunnel pipes carried the fresh, sparkling water to the public fountains of the town. Athens too had to supplement its wells and springs with an underground aqueduct during the sixth century B.C.

A century later, when the ten-mile-long conduit which served the city of Olynthus was built, some of its water was even diverted into a few privileged houses on its way to the public fountain. This was exceptional. Private houses sometimes had wells of questionable purity or cisterns to collect rain, but drinking water was normally fetched from a communal fountain placed over a natural spring or fed by underground pipes. The fountains became great social centres. Women gossiped and exchanged the latest news as they waited to fill their pitchers at the continuously gushing spouts.

A vase-painting showing Greek girls collecting water from a fountain.

Rome, founded in 753 B.C., was eventually served by the most comprehensive water supply system of ancient times, although for the first four centuries of its existence its citizens made do with water from the Tiber or from local springs and wells. It was not until 312 B.C. that the first aqueduct was built to augment natural supplies. Following the Greek pattern this was underground, and the ten-mile-long channel carrying pure spring water emerged into the open only for the last hundred yards of its journey.

In 272 B.C. a second aqueduct was built. This time the channel ran for about forty miles beneath the surface carrying clear water all the way from Tivoli. More than a century passed before another aqueduct was required. This was completed in 140 B.C. and was the first to be carried overhead for any distance on the bridge-like structures which now seem typical of Roman aqueducts. Seven miles of the fifty-seven-mile-long watercourse were actually above the ground.

Although many additional aqueducts were subsequently constructed, this third one, the Marcia as it was called, always occupied a special place in the affections of the Roman people. Its waters were the sweetest and the coolest. All Rome was shocked when the Emperor Nero swam in its sacred source spring, and nobody was surprised or sorry that this escapade was followed by an almost fatal bout of rheumatic fever.

By the middle of the first century A.D. Rome had nine aqueducts, and a further four were added before all the conduits were cut during the siege of Rome by the Goths in A.D. 537. In its prime the Roman water system delivered perhaps forty gallons of water every day for each of the city's million inhabitants, but little of this supply was piped into private premises. Most went to the ever popular bathing establishments and to the public fountains or water basins, which, according to a fourth-century survey, numbered 1,352. Piped water was a luxury available only to those wealthy enough to own a private house or live in one of the expensive suites that occupied the ground floors of some of Rome's tall apartment blocks.

Other cities in the Roman Empire had water supply systems similar to the capital's, although, of course, on a much smaller scale. Ruins of about two hundred aqueducts have been discovered, but most of these splendid structures were destroyed or allowed to fall into disrepair after the barbarians overran the Western Empire in the fifth century A.D.

Only in the East where Roman power continued to flourish did efficient water distribution survive. Even today one of the aqueducts which served Constantinople still stands in a good state of preservation in modern Istanbul. Warned by the example of Rome's severed aqueducts, the citizens of Constantinople realized that complete reliance on vulnerable conduits put them at the mercy of any attacker. Their answer to this problem was to dig huge underground reservoirs in which to store water against an emergency. Thirty or more of these cisterns have been discovered, but two built in the sixth century at the orders of the Emperor Justinian are the most impressive — the many pillars supporting their roofs 63

A nineteenth-century engraving of Valens Aqueduct in Istanbul which was completed
in A.D. 378.

A Byzantine cistern under modern Istanbul.

giving them the appearance of submerged cathedrals. One is still used as a reservoir to the present day.

In Europe the glories of Roman water engineering were forgotten, and townsmen turned once again to rivers and local springs. While settlements were small this was tolerable, but as towns grew their rivers became steadily more polluted. Wells and springs were unable to meet the increased demand, so that by the thirteenth century pure water was always in short supply in the larger cities. John Stow, writing in the sixteenth century about the London of three hundred years before, had this to say: "... the fresh waters that were in and about this city, being in process of time, by encroachment for buildings, and otherwise heightening of grounds, utterly decayed, and the number of citizens mightily increased, they were forced to seek sweet waters abroad."

In 1236 the landowner Gilbert Sanfolds allowed the people of London to lay a six inch lead pipe or conduit across his property to bring water from the Tyburn springs into the city at Cheapside. London, in its efforts to solve its water problem, was following the example set long before by 65

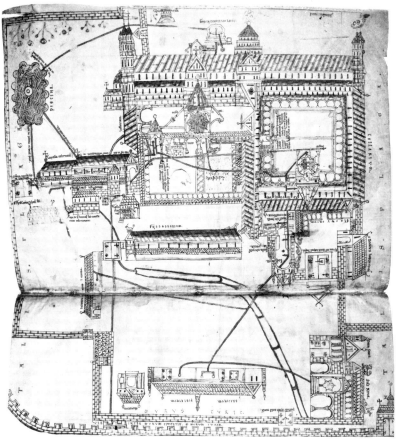

A plan of the twelfth-century water supply systems at Canterbury from the Canterbury psalter.

the monasteries. The monastic orders had never quite lost touch with the old civilization, and had a Roman regard for cleanliness. As far back as the ninth century the brothers of the Abbaye of St Laurent at Paris had diverted water so as to make it flow into their buildings. Exact plans still exist for the later water system built in 1160 by the monks of Canterbury, who used lead pipes to carry spring water on a three-quarter-mile journey over the moat, through the town wall, and into the monastery.

Water supplied through a conduit pipe had many advantages. It could be brought to a convenient point within the town walls; it flowed from its outlet just at the right height to be collected in a bucket without the irksome winding necessary at a well; most important of all it was almost totally free from the danger of pollution. Expense was the only major drawback. The initial cost of laying pipes from the spring persuaded many poorer towns to seek the charity of a neighbouring religious foundation.

Many towns did, in fact, gain a water supply from outside their walls through the generosity of churchmen. Monks at Southampton began to share their piped water with the townsmen in 1310, and during the course of the fourteenth century such other English cities as Chester, Grantham, and Lincoln benefited in the same way from the enterprise of local monasteries.

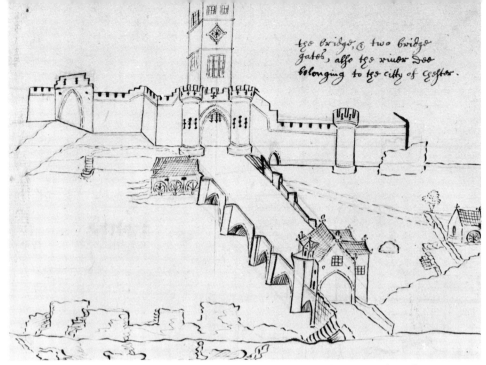

the bridge, & two bridge gates, also the river Dee belonging to the citty of Chester.

A seventeenth-century drawing showing waterwheels pumping river water into the town of Chester.

Richer or more go-ahead town communities helped themselves. Dublin built a conduit during the middle years of the thirteenth century, while Hull during the same century avoided the expense of lead pipes or an underground tunnel by diverting a spring into the bed of an existing stream. Perhaps the most elaborate water system of that period, however, belonged to the Belgian city of Bruges. Each important street junction had its own fountain or basin fed by subterranean conduits supplied from a reservoir outside the town.

Gradually the use of conduits spread, but although they eased the problem of water shortage they were never intended to provide ordinary citizens with the luxury of running water in their homes. The king, the monks, and a few favoured noblemen had water piped into their houses. The mass of people fetched theirs from the fountain or brought it from a water seller. Occasionally unscrupulous and ingenious townsmen tried to avoid this inconvenience by tapping the public conduit with an illegal pipe of their own. A record of 1478 describes how one Londoner, William Campion, was punished for such an offence by being paraded through the streets on horseback while water cascaded all over him from a perforated vessel perched on his head.

The waterworks on London Bridge.

By the end of the Middle Ages some cities already needed more water than spring-fed conduits could deliver, but fortunately the Germans found a solution to the problem. Pumps, worked by wheels set in the arches of bridges, sucked up river water and forced it into underground pipes which led to the city fountains. An almost unlimited supply could be provided, though not without a serious loss in purity. Breslau was drawing on river water in this way as early as 1479, and during the sixteenth and seventeenth centuries waterworks appeared in many European towns. Paris built its first in 1608, lagging a little behind London which in 1582 had imported a Dutchman, Peter Morice, to install water lifting machinery. Morice was given a five-hundred-year lease on one of the arches of London Bridge, and built a waterwheel pump so powerful that it could throw a jet of water over a church steeple. Besides supplying public fountains, Morice circulated water through lead or elm-wood pipes to the houses of those prepared to pay a water rate. Only the immediate neighbourhood was served at first, but the company gradually extended its network of pipes and survived until 1822 when increasing river pollution forced Parliament to close it down.

The use of water-powered pumps marked the beginning of the supply of water to private houses, but those fortunate enough to obtain piped water were not expected to abuse the privilege. Early-seventeenth-century private supplies could easily be forfeited as even the aristocratic Essex family discovered, when in 1608 the Lord Mayor punished them for wastefulness by cutting off the water to their London residence.

During the course of the seventeenth century, however, the pace of progress quickened, and many provincial cities set up waterworks to carry water into the homes of their more prosperous citizens. The poor expected and received no such luxury. They continued to rely on public conduits, or bought water from the water sellers, who remained active down to the middle of the nineteenth century.

American towns were for the most part small enough to make do with wells and springs until the middle of the eighteenth century, although a number of Boston householders had piped water into their homes from the Jamaica Pond about a hundred years earlier. The first public water-works in the United States was built at Bethlehem, Pennsylvania, in 1755.

London was probably the best watered city during the 1700s. A Swiss visitor of 1726, M. de Saussure, wrote enthusiastically that ". . . everyone can have an abundance of water," though he also noted that the pipes gave only "three hours water in every twenty-four." Cisterns were filled during these three hours, and the store of water had to suffice for the rest of the day.

Other cities had similar restrictions, but various technical improvements gradually increased the supply. Newly invented steam engines were set to work to pump river-water into the distribution pipes. First to try the experiment was London's York Buildings waterworks, which began to use steam-power to raise water from the River Thames in 1720. The steam engine was still working during M. de Saussure's stay, but its fuel bill was too great for it to be an economic success. It was not until 1784 that an improved unit invented by John Smeaton allowed the York Buildings to reintroduce steam-power on a commercial basis.

Once it had been demonstrated that steam pumps could pay their way, other waterworks began to employ them. The Watering Committee of Philadelphia installed the first one in the United States in 1797, while six years later France followed suit and constructed a steam engine to lift water into the aqueduct at the Marly works near Paris.   69

York House waterworks in the late eighteenth century.

Another innovation was the use of iron water mains, which were far less prone to wasteful leakage than the older wooden pipes. The earliest known iron water-pipe was the fifteen-mile-long aqueduct built late in the seventeenth century to carry water from Marly to Versailles. Fifty years passed, however, before iron mains began to find favour within cities. Edinburgh replaced some of its lead pipes with iron in 1755, and Dublin probably started to use iron in 1776. The more general adoption of iron mains came at the beginning of the nineteenth century. In 1817 the British Parliament ruled that within ten years no new main would be allowed unless it were made of iron, and also in 1817 the first iron pipes to be used in the United States were laid down in Philadelphia. Strangely enough, however, timber pipes were still carrying water into some major American cities well into the twentieth century. In some western states, where timber was plentiful and iron expensive, large wooden pipes made of staves bound together with steel hoops were used as aqueducts. Denver

Schuylkill Waterworks, Philadelphia about 1840.

and Salt Lake City were two communities which relied on such wooden pipes until the inter-wars period.

Throughout the eighteenth and into the first years of the nineteenth century, people were concerned more with increasing the availability of water in cities than with assuring the quality of what was delivered. As industrialization got under way and towns mushroomed, river pollution became much more serious. The building of sewers aggravated rather than solved the problem, because tainted material found its way into the streams and rivers more quickly than before. Completely untreated sewage flowed into rivers, often within feet of where water was pumped out for drinking purposes. Not surprisingly, water-borne diseases like cholera raged through the cities of Europe and America during the mid-nineteenth century. Cholera claimed 14,000 victims in London alone during the single year of 1849.

By the 1820s, thirty years before it was proved scientifically that polluted water could spread disease, complaints were already being voiced about the state of urban water supplies. A pamphlet of 1827 criticized London's water as being "offensive to the sight, disgusting to the imagination and destructive to the health," while artist William Heath's vision of the 71

The Harlem River Bridge on the Croton Aqueduct in about 1850.

contents of Thames water must have made many people wonder just what they were drinking.

A great improvement was made in 1829 when James Simpson, the engineer of the Chelsea and Lambeth Water Companies of London, devised a method for filtering water through successive layers of sand, gravel, and stones. In this way, gross impurities were completely removed, and bacterial contamination was greatly reduced. The British Government, by an Act of 1852, made it illegal for water companies to supply unfiltered river-water. Filtration and chlorination, a supplementary protection introduced in 1908, have now given many western cities a completely safe water supply, though this is far from true of the developing countries.

New York was the first modern city to supply itself with an abundance of pure water. Between 1837 and 1842 Croton Creek was dammed to make a reservoir, and a $38\frac{1}{4}$-mile-long aqueduct, running mainly underground, was constructed to deliver ninety-five million gallons of water to the city every day.

New York set an example which other cities have since attempted to follow. However, there are difficulties, as New York itself learned during the drought of 1965. Increasing populations mean that cities have to reach out further to find sufficient water. Los Angeles has even found it necessary to build a 440-mile-long aqueduct to tap the waters of the Sacramento River, while New York's new Delaware aqueduct is over 120 miles in length.

In industrialized countries water is often used more than once as it flows to the sea. Towns lower down river receive water which has already been drawn in and then expelled as sewage by upstream communities. It is estimated that 60 per cent of the 150 million Americans supplied by waterworks drink "second-" or even "third-hand" water. But for filtration and chlorination, water-borne diseases would be endemic.

In developing nations, where many towns have grown too fast for technical improvements to keep pace with population increase, conditions are reminiscent of early nineteenth-century Europe. Up to one third of the town dwellers of India and South America have no private supply of water. Calcutta, the centre of cholera infection, drank until recently the unfiltered waters of the filthy River Hooghly, and in the slums even the doubtful privilege of access to a tap had to be shared with upwards of thirty other people. The World Health Organization has helped Calcutta to chlorinate the unfiltered part of its water supply, but despite efforts of this sort and loans from richer countries, too many towns still have inadequate or positively dangerous water.

5

The Disposal of Wastes

Rubbish and sewage are inevitable by-products of living, so that whenever large populations collect together in cities the disposal of waste becomes a problem. Nomads can move on if they foul a campsite; city dwellers must live with their mess or learn how to remove it. Ironically, the more civilization develops, the greater the problems become. In the course of a single day a modern United States city of a million inhabitants produces two thousand tons of solid refuse, pollutes its atmosphere with almost a thousand tons of soot and noxious chemicals, and pours out half a million tons of sewage. Without the painfully acquired expertise in waste disposal gained by past generations of townsmen, contemporary cities would succumb beneath a mountain of filth.

Even the nomadic Hebrews of Old Testament times observed rules of hygiene. In Deuteronomy XXIII they were instructed:

"Thou shalt have a place also without the camp, whither thou shalt go forth abroad:
And thou shalt have a paddle upon thy weapon; and it shall be, when thou wilt ease thyself abroad, thou shalt dig therewith, and shalt turn back and cover that which cometh from thee."

Possibly early agricultural villagers adopted similar measures to manure their fields and keep their settlements sweet. As communities grew in size, however, such simple expedients became impracticable. Dung heaps and piles of refuse collected inexorably — festering sores in the fabric of the city.

The ancient Sumerian cities made no attempt to dispose of household refuse. Shells, bones, and scraps of food were thrown unceremoniously into the road where they remained to rot unless carried off by a dog or some other scavenger. Gradually the level of the ground was raised by these practices until each city perched on a low hill of ancestral rubbish.

Most Sumerians were almost as casual in their disposal of sewage, but the kings and eventually the wealthier citizens learned to be more parti-

Third millennium B.C. sewer under the ruined city of Eshnunna.

Open drain running down an alley in Mohenjo-daro.

cular. Several palaces of the latter part of the third millennium B.C. had water-flushed lavatories and effective drains. At one royal residence in the city of Eshnunna the excavators even found the remains of the large jars which had stood beside each privy to provide water for flushing. By the second millennium the sanitary idea had caught on with the middle classes. Houses of that period, unearthed by Sir Leonard Woolley in a well-to-do quarter of Ur, had lavatories connected to underground terracotta sewers. Such luxuries remained unknown, however, in poorer city districts.

In ancient Egypt conditions never rose above the primitive. Refuse was tossed away to moulder in the streets. Stinking piles of garbage provided breeding grounds for swarms of flies, and it is known from the evidence of medical papyri that many Egyptian city dwellers suffered from the fly-borne diseases, trachoma and ophthalmia. As rainfall was scanty, the Egyptians did not need to dig underground drains for their towns, so sewers to carry away waste materials never had a chance to develop. Even the mighty Pharaoh had to make do with an earth closet and his poorer subjects probably made do with nothing at all.

The Indus Valley civilization, which flourished from about 2300 to 1700 B.C., paid far more attention to waste disposal. Its major cities, 75

The Cloaca Maxima as it looked in the nineteenth century.

Mohenjo-daro and Harappā, had carefully built channels to drain both streets and buildings, and many homes boasted water-flushed lavatories. At intervals along the streets stood brick bins, each located beneath a chute in the wall of a house. It is thought that rubbish and domestic left-overs were thrown down the chutes to await collection by what were possibly the world's first dustmen.

The Greek civilization, for all its many accomplishments, could not compare with the Indus culture in the sphere of city hygiene. Sanitation was almost completely lacking in Greek cities, and refuse disposal was mainly the concern of the dogs. Disease was an inevitable consequence of this neglect. All Greek towns suffered to some extent, but for Athens the reckoning was particularly bitter. In 430 B.C., at the beginning of the desperate Peloponnesian War, the city was paralysed by a terrifying plague. Citizens died in swarms, law and custom broke down, and the Athenian war-effort was seriously undermined.

Rome did at least make some effort to keep itself clean. By the time of the Emperors it possessed an excellent sewer system, which had slowly evolved from earlier drains built to carry away surface water. The principal sewer, the Cloaca Maxima, typically began as an open ditch dug during the sixth century B.C. to drain the marshy area of what was to become the Forum. It was probably two hundred years before the channel was vaulted over to make it a true underground sewer. In the second century B.C. the Cloaca was reconstructed and paved with such long-lasting blocks of lava that it stayed in use as a sewer until the beginning of the present century. Rome even had a goddess of the drains — Venus Cloacina, the protectress of the unfortunate slaves whose job it was to dredge the sewers.

Despite Rome's magnificent drains few of its citizens enjoyed the privilege of a private, water-flushed lavatory. Only the homes of the wealthy were connected to the sewer network. Poorer people, living in tenement blocks, either went out to a public lavatory where a small charge was made or resorted to an evil-smelling, communal privy on the ground floor of their own dwelling. These privies emptied into cesspits, which had to fill up to the top before their contents were removed and carted out of town for use as fertilizer.

Refuse was also carried out of the city, but there was then the problem of what to do with it. Rome's solution was far from satisfactory. Great pits, up to thirty feet deep were dug just outside the walls and left open to receive animal, vegetable, and even human remains. A pestilential smell was still evident when some of the pits were opened up for investigation in the nineteenth century. In use they must have stunk almost unbearably, and posed a serious and continuing threat to public health.

Roman sewers were not confined to the capital alone. The legions carried a regard for sanitation to the most far flung corners of the Empire. Lavatories emptying into a sewer have been discovered at the baths which the Romans built at Silchester in their most northerly province, Britain.

At the other end of their dominions, where the new capital, Constantinople, was founded in A.D. 330, great care was taken to lay down a satisfactory drainage system as a prelude to development. Huge sewers discharged straight into the sea, but their use was as limited as in Rome. Only the better quality houses had water-flushed lavatories.

With the fall of the Roman Empire in the West, efficient sanitation disappeared from most of Europe. Many towns were depopulated, and primitive methods of sewage disposal sufficed in the smaller settlements which took their place. Farmyard practices remained tolerable even after the urban way of life began to revive during the eleventh century. Large cities were a rarity throughout the medieval period, so there was no overwhelming compulsion to re-acquire the lost arts of sanitation.

It was not that medieval city dwellers were totally oblivious of filth and its dangers. Many of the lesser people were ignorant or lazy, but the town 77 authorities at least did not suffer dirt gladly. The will to make cities clean was often there; the knowledge of how to achieve cleanliness was at first lacking. Gradually organization improved and municipal laws aimed against the accumulation of rubbish and sewage became more effective.

The great problem was removal. There were no sewers and in earlier times no organized collections of refuse. Many people threw their garbage higgledy-piggledy into the streets, while others allowed huge muck heaps to mount unchecked until they obstructed the highway. As standards advanced such blatantly selfish conduct was no longer countenanced. This change in public attitude was shown by the increasing number of offenders brought before the courts. William Wigger of St Ives, England, for one, was fined sixpence in 1302 for possessing an outsized garbage heap. Smaller piles of rubbish were of necessity still permitted, but towns eventually put a limit on the time refuse could lie undisturbed by the roadside. In the middle of the fourteenth century Londoners had seven days grace before they had to move their heaps. By 1421 Coventry had cut the time to a night and a day, while five decades before, the proud citizens of York had forbidden the accumulation of any heap at all. Cities were getting themselves organized.

In most towns it became the custom for each family to clean the street in front of its house. London and Bristol adopted this practice in the fourteenth century, and early in the fifteenth, Coventry threatened a twelve-penny fine, quite a sum in those days, for any citizen who neglected to sweep his stretch each Saturday. Not all cities were so vigilant, for the difficulties were discouraging. The pigs, goats, horses, and cattle, which were kept in every town, added enormously to the mess in the streets, while from a mixture of ignorance and necessity many citizens persisted in surreptitiously dumping rubbish in the thoroughfares. Civic pride battled with sloth and indifference, and often lost. On the whole complete reliance on self-help did not prove an effective method of keeping a city clean.

Larger towns began to employ professional sweepers to help keep the litter in check. London certainly had some as early as 1299, when one of their number, a rascal named Strago, finished up in prison for maligning the city officials. Town dust carts also made a belated appearance, and provided citizens with a much needed means of removing the muck heaps from their doorsteps. In the closing years of the fourteenth century London had a fleet of twelve vehicles, and each parish was allotted a special day for refuse collection. By 1407 the service was working well enough for the authorities to insist that rubbish be kept off the streets until a wagon was due to pass by. Many towns, however, clung to the old ways of doing things and left each citizen to dispose of his own rubbish as best he could. In such places roadside dung heaps had to be endured until long after the Middle Ages had passed.

Even when cities had organized refuse removal there was still the problem of what to do with the rubbish once it had been collected. The old solution of throwing it over the town wall or dumping it in the nearest river became less acceptable as time progressed. River water was used on a vast scale for brewing, and no town would willingly allow its streams to be polluted. In 1369, for instance, London decreed that its butchers could no longer dispose of their offal into the Thames. Cities started to set aside special sites where rubbish could legally be tipped. London instituted dumping areas in the latter part of the fourteenth century to be followed sooner or later by most other major British towns. In this way stench and ugliness were localized and cities were protected from a ring of rubbish growing up around their walls. It was not an ideal method of disposal, but it was the best the age could contrive.

Perhaps the most unsatisfactory aspect of medieval city life was the absence of any proper means of removing sewage. Even in the castles of the nobility where the lavatories or garderobes often discharged into the already stagnant waters of the moat, the sanitary arrangements were inadequate. Townsmen were certainly no better provided for than their masters. Human wastes must have found their way into many a garbage heap or have been emptied into the streets to lie in the open drainage channels until the next rainstorm washed them away. About the best a householder could do was dig a pit in the garden and build a lavatory above it. Even this could get him into trouble if a neighbour objected to the smell. Regulations dealing with this difficulty were issued to Londoners as early as 1189. No one, it was decreed, should dig an unwalled cesspool closer than five-and-a-half feet from the boundary line with his neighbour.

Privies were also built above watercourses, reducing to open sewers the streams on which many citizens still relied for water. Despite their rules against offal dumping, city authorities were often as much to blame for this as private individuals. Public latrines were not infrequently cleaned by a gush of river water passing underneath. It was not until towards the end of medieval times that municipalities recognized that sewage intro-duced into streams in this way was as serious a pollutant as garbage and rubbish. London, in 1477, issued a general ban on lavatories built over the city's minor waterways, but was probably never able to enforce it. Medieval technology just could not cope with urban sewage problems.   79

Towns in the Middle Ages had always been cushioned by their small size from the worst consequences of their hygienic deficiencies. With the exception of the Black Death, which killed perhaps a third of the population of Europe in the fourteenth century, the epidemics were no more serious than in nineteenth-century industrial communities. The Renaissance brought a growth in city populations without any compensating improvements in the techniques of waste removal. More buildings were crammed into the often inadequate area ringed by the old town walls. Overcrowding defeated the good intentions of the authorities, so that the poorer citizens were condemned to live in squalor. The Renaissance genius, Leonardo da Vinci (1452–1519), was considered eccentric in suggesting that all lavatories should drain into underground sewers. To most Europeans of that time, smell, filth, and disease were the inevitable penalty to be paid for the pleasure of living together in cities.

Their contemporaries, the technological primitive Aztecs of Mexico, adopted a more positive approach. Although Cortez, who landed near Vera Cruz in the last year of Leonardo's life, was able to overthrow the whole empire with a handful of men, the Aztecs still had something to teach their conquerors. Tenochtitlán, the capital, was built on an island in a lake, and was connected to the mainland by causeways. A hundred thousand people lived in the island city, which was intersected by many canals. The health risk was enormous, yet the Aztecs remained in control of the situation. Special boats were moored along the canal banks to serve as public lavatories. Once full, they were towed away and their contents used to manure the land. After the Spanish conquest this simple but effective method of sanitation fell into disuse, and disease swept through the city.

The bad old ways persisted in Europe throughout the seventeenth century and well on into the eighteenth. Open sewer streams, as foul as anything from the Middle Ages, still trickled down the streets of sophisticated Stuart London, while the contents of slop buckets continued to cascade from upper windows onto the luckless heads below. It was only about the middle of the eighteenth century that conditions began to improve. Streets were widened in many towns, and what sewers existed were at last covered over. Significantly such improvements were accompanied by a decrease in the death rate.

By the early years of the nineteenth century the need for sewers was more widely recognized, and new drains were constructed beneath important cities like London and Paris in Europe and New York and Boston in America. At first only favoured localities were served, as for

Hogarth's engraving shows that the chamber-pot was still a danger in the streets of eighteenth-century London.

instance the famous Strand in London along which a sewer was laid in 1801. Those who were lucky enough to live near a sewer could run drains into it for a fee, but most townspeople still had to make do with cesspits that not infrequently lurked under their living rooms. The nightman with his buckets and cart remained indispensable. Even where sewers had been built, they all too often discharged into the very streams that were used to supply drinking water.

Step by step the situation improved as public opinion was gradually won over to the cause of cleanliness. A crucial turning point came with the report of the Health of Towns Commission in 1844. The respectable British middle class was shocked to the core by the account of widespread misery and squalor amongst industrial workers, and thereafter gave the so-called "sanitary" movement their support. Expert advice was not lacking. Already, in 1842, the reformer Edwin Chadwick had laid before Parliament his answer to the problem of sewage disposal. Each street was to be sewered, and all houses were to be connected to the water mains. Waste water poured down household sinks would then serve the useful purpose of keeping the sewage moving along the underground drains.

From the mid-nineteenth century, England began to set an example which was followed by the rest of the world. Under the direction of the engineer Sir Joseph Bazalgette London started work in 1856 on a huge, interconnecting sewer system. Enough had been constructed by 1865 to enable a formal opening by the Prince of Wales, later Edward VII, but the entire network took a further ten years to complete. When finished it was the largest and most modern system of its day. Its eighty-three miles of main sewer served an area of over one hundred square miles, and coped efficiently with a daily outfall of 120 million gallons. Unfortunately the system had an extremely serious fault. All this raw sewage was poured untreated into the lower reaches of the Thames, which were polluted to an unprecedented extent. Nevertheless the sewers brought about a quick improvement in London's health record. The death-rate showed a distinct drop in the 1870s.

New York's sewer system had the same basic defect as that of London. It too discharged untreated sewage into the waterways. By the second decade of the twentieth century pollution had reached such a serious level that filtering stations were set up, but even today a considerable portion of New York City's daily 1,000 million gallons of sewage goes untreated into the harbour.

Although effective methods of sewage purification were evolved in the last part of the nineteenth century, New York is not alone in its pollution

Part of London's main sewer system built by Sir Joseph Bazalgette.

problems. Throughout the United States and Europe many cities still pump sewage straight into rivers, lakes, or the sea. Unbelievably, there are two thousand communities in the United States alone with absolutely no sewage treatment installations. The price of unpolluted waters is more than city authorities are willing or able to pay.

Sewage disposal is not the only problem. The old question of what to do with solid rubbish still plagues the modern city. Nowadays there is more than ever to throw away, and no town can afford to be without a refuse removal service. The present relative efficiency of collection, if not always of final disposal, is a development of the nineteenth century.

New York can furnish an example of the gradual improvement in city cleansing which occurred during the nineteenth century. At the outset conditions were extremely primitive. The English traveller William Cobbett, who visited New York in 1817, wrote scathingly of garbage flung into the streets to be devoured by "the street hogs, a thousand or two of which are constantly fattening." Evidently the hogs were still around during Charles Dickens' stay of 1842 for in his "American Notes" he warned visitors to "take care of the pigs." In 1866 the responsibility for keeping the city clean was given to the Metropolitan Board of Health, but within six years this body had passed the problem to the Board of Police. Naturally enough refuse collection ranked low in the list of police priorities, and New York streets stayed filthy. Such an unsatisfactory arrangement could not last for long, and in 1881 a Department of Street Cleaning was formed with its own commissioner. Even then the service left much to be desired. According to Jacob Riis, the photographer and campaigner for social justice, it was not until Commissioner George Waring took over in 1895 that the Department at last removed ". . . the ash barrels which had befouled the sidewalks . . ."

Nowadays all major cities organize refuse collection, and special vehicles, usually owned by the municipality, make regular calls in each neighbourhood. There still remains, however, the problem of what to do with the accumulated rubbish. In the past, many large coastal or river cities merely took their refuse out to sea and dumped it. Much floated back inshore to contaminate other people's beaches, so that this practice has been largely discontinued. New York gave up sea dumping in 1936 on the orders of the United States Supreme Court. Land dumps are also undesirable. They look ugly, smell bad, and are the breeding grounds for flies and disease. Only if the rubbish is deposited in trenches and covered over the same day with a seal of packed down earth does the method become acceptable.

84   Many British and American cities dispose of their refuse in this way. Other

This Jacob Riis photograph shows a New York street shortly before the great clean-up organized by George Waring.

communities use incineration to reduce their collected rubbish to an inoffensive ash.

Yet incineration itself, while solving one problem, adds to another—air pollution over the cities. Modern civilization needs an ever increasing supply of energy to power its factories, drive its cars, and light and heat its homes. Most of this energy comes directly or indirectly from the combustion of some form of fuel. Great quantities of coke, oil, and petroleum are burned, inevitably releasing ash and noxious chemicals into the atmosphere. Usually winds and natural convection currents ensure that the air change over a city is rapid enough to prevent pollution reaching a dangerous concentration. Occasionally, however, the atmosphere remains so still that lethal fogs develop. Sixty-three people died in 1930, when smoke from Liège built up in the Meuse Valley of Belgium, while an incredibly dense fog which enveloped London for several days in December 1952 killed about four thousand chest-sufferers. Air pollution is a very real danger.

One of George Waring's New York street sweepers.

Smoke from domestic fires must always have been something of a nuisance, but the problem only became serious when coal began to replace wood as a fuel. In 1257 England's Edward I threatened death to anyone caught burning coal after his queen had been driven from Nottingham Castle by sulphurous fumes rising from the town below. Necessity, however, knows no master, and as the forests grew thinner and firewood scarcer, more and more coal was burned. The Industrial Revolution worsened the situation beyond all measure. Smoke from factory chimneys

86

Air pollution became a problem in the nineteenth century.

and thousands of household hearths hung heavily over the grimy towns of the new machine age. A choking, poisonous atmosphere seemed part of the price of progress. "Where there's muck, there's money" became the watch word.

Not everyone adopted such a complacent attitude. In 1819 a British Parliamentary committee mulled over the problem of air pollution without achieving any positive results, but the later committees of 1843 and 1845 were more effective. Shortly after their deliberations, Acts were passed to reduce the smoke emitted by locomotives and factories. The British Public Health Act of 1875 again gave powers to deal with excessive factory smoke, but one of the most persistent polluters of the atmosphere, the domestic coal fire, was ignored.

In the United States, too, industrialization made air pollution a matter for concern. St Louis was the first American city to take smoke seriously. In the mid-nineteenth century it set a minimum height for chimneys, and in 1864 its courts awarded damages to a plaintiff who alleged nuisance by smoke. Slightly later Chicago took up the cause of smoke abatement. A citizens' association began agitation in 1874, and in 1881 the Chicago city council branded all emission of dense smoke a nuisance punishable by fine. Other mid-western towns followed suit.

Most nineteenth-century smoke abatement policies were aimed against factories. In the twentieth century legislation has also encompassed the domestic hearth, and has begun to extend to a newer source of pollution — the automobile. The British Clean Air Act of 1956 included even England's long cherished coal fires. Smokeless zones were established and

Smog in Los Angeles.

gradually extended, in which open fires were only allowed if modified to burn coke or some other improved fuel. Non-industrial suburbs now have a noticeably purer atmosphere, and really dense fogs are much less common than formerly.

National clean air legislation was enacted in the United States in 1963. The Act promised "federal financial assistance . . . to prevent and control air pollution," and called for periodic reports on appliances which reduced the toxic content of automobile exhaust gases. Unburnt fuel and poisonous carbon monoxide in the exhausts expelled by automobile engines have become a major pollution problem in modern cities. California, whose towns have suffered notoriously from car-smog, has been the pioneer state in tackling this difficulty. Since 1966 every new vehicle sold within the state boundaries must by law be fitted with an exhaust control device. For the future there is even some thought of finding a new, cleaner type of motor to replace the car's internal combustion engine. The air can be made purer if society is willing to foot the bill for more refined fuels and modified automobiles.

Over the centuries cities have learned to rid themselves of most of their wastes, but a new problem has arisen out of their very success. In this age of giant cities too little thought has been given to the cumulative effects of the huge quantities of sewage and industrial effluent poured into the inland waterways. Today's cities are keeping themselves clean only at the
expense of poisoning their surrounding environments.

6

The City's Protectors

Every community needs security. Ancient cities surrounded themselves with walls to keep out warlike intruders, but such defences offered no protection from the internal ravages of fire and crime. Organized protective services were required if these evils were to be kept effectively in check.

As far as is known fire-fighting was a communal effort in early cities all over the world. Everyone turned out to lend a hand, but enthusiasm could not make up for indiscipline and lack of equipment. Water had to be carried from the nearest river or well in buckets, and it was difficult to get close enough to throw the water onto the flames. Once a blaze had really taken hold it stayed alight until it had burnt itself out.

The cities of Sumeria, although without fire brigades, probably did recruit policemen to preserve internal law and order. Ur Nammu, king of Ur from 2113 to 2096 B.C. and eventual ruler over all Mesopotamia, issued the first written collection of laws in history, and boasted that he had rid the land of criminals. Neither laws nor boast would have been worth the clay they were written on without the backing of some form of police organization.

In the famous code of justice of a later Sumerian law-giver, Hammurabi, who lived in the eighteenth century B.C., appeared the word "rêdum," translated by scholars as "gendarme" and taken to be the first direct mention ever made of a police official. It remained for the Bible, however, to give a possible glimpse of the Sumerian police service in action. While the Patriarch Abraham was encamped in the land of the two rivers, his elderly wife Sarah's jealousy of the Egyptian maid Hagar erupted into a violent quarrel. Heartbroken, the young girl ran away, only to be discovered at a well in the desert by a kindly "angel of the Lord," who promptly sent her back home. "Angel," it must be remembered, means "messenger," and the questions—"Whence camest thou? and whither wilt thou go?"—asked by this one make him seem more a police officer, 89

Part of a stone engraved with Hammurabi's law code. The King is shown receiving the laws from the seated sun god.

a messenger of the king, than a servant of God.

The script used by the Indus people still defies translation, so any evidence for the policing of their cities must come from the ruins they left behind. One building in Mohenjo-daro has been dubbed a police station by some archaeologists because of the cell-like rooms it contains, but stronger proof for the existence of a watch-keeping force is provided by the

Scythian archers like these shown on a fourth-century B.C. vase acted as Athens' first police force.

sentry boxes dotted around the town.

In Egypt policemen were chosen from amongst the Nubians who were noted for their imposing physiques. Crime could not have seemed very attractive to the slightly built Egyptians faced with such burly opposition.

By Greek time more definite facts begin to emerge of the ways in which towns protected themselves against their lawless elements. Most ancient Greek cities relied on citizen arrest. Each individual had the powers of a modern policeman, and was expected to exercise them if he saw the law flouted. This worked so long as the Greeks retained their early devotion to the institutions of their city-states, but as growth and prosperity weakened the feelings of communal unity the citizen police systems began to collapse. By the late seventh century B.C. Athens, for instance, was a violent, dangerous city, with its people divided into factions. Something had to be done, but instead of organizing a professional police force the Athenians chose to alter their laws to make punishments sterner. In about 621 B.C. Draco prepared a penal system so harsh that it is still a by-word for severity. Nearly every offence carried the death sentence, but the crime wave continued unabated. Few criminals were arrested, and those who were often escaped justice because of the very harshness of the new laws. Courts hesitated to convict even the obviously guilty except for a particularly brutal crime. Solon (638 to c.558 B.C.) reformed the laws again, but Athens continued to close its mind to the only effective solution to its internal disorders. Until the rise to power of the dictator Peisistratus, the city remained without police.

Peisistratus, who lived from about 605 to 527 B.C., returned to Athens in 541 B.C. after spending a prolonged exile building up a personal army. Once in office the new dictator gave some of his mercenaries the task of keeping the peace in his turbulent capital. His troop of Scythian archers became the first disciplined police force that Athens had ever known. After Peisistratus' death, however, the old ways reasserted themselves. The Scythians were downgraded from real policemen to ceremonial guards, whose main function was to act as ushers in the assembly.

Sparta, alone amongst its neighbours, maintained a police force as part of its state machinery. The oppression which its small citizen class exercised over the much larger helot population made coercion a necessity. From early in its history Sparta employed an efficient and sinister secret police to quietly engineer the permanent disappearance of anyone who dared to spread the seed of discontent.

Ironically enough, the Greeks, who in general disapproved of organized police forces, later provided the recruits for what was perhaps the most

91

effective police system in the ancient world. Alexander the Great (356 to 323 B.C.) spread Greek influence as far as northern India by his conquests, but on his death his short-lived empire broke into fragments. Ptolemy, one of Alexander's generals, seized Egypt, and to consolidate his power encouraged Greeks to emigrate to his new country. All young men amongst these newcomers were liable to military service, but those not immediately required by the army were drafted to the police. Skilful use of this tool helped keep the dynasty of the Ptolemies in power until Egypt came under Roman sway in 30 B.C. The first emperor of Rome, Augustus, is in fact thought to have modelled the combined police and fire brigade that he instituted in his own capital on the much admired force which existed in the great Egyptian city of Alexandria. Certainly the Roman firemen made use of one invaluable Alexandrian invention, the pump devised by Ctesibius in the third century B.C.

Before Augustus' time the Romans had applied surprisingly little of their great organizational ability to the protection of their own extremely vulnerable city. The rapid rebuilding of Rome after its destruction by the Gauls in 389 B.C. had left it a maze of narrow alleys – a happy hunting ground for the criminal and an appalling fire risk. To control this great rabbit warren of a city there was only one tiny corps of trained police, the "questores paricidii," whose job it was to track down murderers. Otherwise, the police power still lay in the hands of an increasingly apathetic populace, demoralized and divided by civil wars. Crime went virtually unchecked, and fire-fighting was almost equally neglected. There were a few professional firemen before the fall of the Republic in the first century B.C., but the service they provided was woefully inadequate.

The most powerful city on earth could not permanently endure such internal chaos. When Augustus emerged from the civil wars as sole ruler and first Emperor of the Roman world, one of his many reforms was the establishment of the long needed police system for his strife-torn capital. Augustus, who formed his corps of "vigiles" in 6 B.C. after watching a disastrous fire, gave the new force the twin task of fighting both flames and crime. Seven cohorts of "vigiles," each one a thousand strong, were recruited and housed in seven police barracks situated at strategic points in the city. To ensure concerted action, the whole force was put under the command of a single prefect of police. The Emperor also instituted three urban cohorts which were part of the army but had special responsibility for suppressing riots.

In their fire-fighting role the "vigiles" carried leather buckets, ladders, ropes, hooks for pulling down burning material, and long-handled mops which when soaked in water were useful for dowsing small fires in inaccessible crannies. Their most sophisticated appliances, portable pumps whose nozzles could be swivelled to squirt a jet of water in any direction, were derived from Ctesibius' invention. The fire department's duties did not end with simply putting out a blaze. Each fire had to be investigated by the prefect of police, who could punish the culprit if any negligence were proved.

Fire brigades were not peculiar to the capital alone. Pumps have been unearthed on the sites of several provincial cities, while correspondence between the Emperor Trajan (*c*.A.D. 56 to 117) and the governor of the province of Bithynia refers in passing to the existence of guilds of firemen in many parts of the Empire.

Two hundred years later, when the Emperor Constantine transformed the little town of Byzantium into Constantinople, a new capital for the ailing Empire, he organized the police and fire services along the same lines as those of Rome. "Vigiles" patrolled the streets at night, while mob violence was suppressed by a special group of mercenary soldiers, under the direct command of the Emperor himself.

Meanwhile the less sophisticated peoples who had overrun Rome's western provinces relied mainly on family groupings to maintain law and order. In Saxon England it was the duty of a man's kindred to avenge him if he were killed by an enemy. On the other side too, all the slayer's kin were involved in the vendetta unless they publicly expelled the wrong-doer from their circle. The only way further bloodshed could be avoided was to pay the injured family a "wergild" — "man-money" — which varied according to the importance of the victim. Sometimes wergild was rejected, and then feuding could drag on for several generations. The kindred also had a responsibility to the community at large. If one of their number was accused of a crime they had to ensure that he appeared before the local assembly, or folk-moot, to defend himself.

Towards the end of the Saxon era the effectiveness of the kindred system began to decline, and new methods of law enforcement started to appear. Men gained increased protection by joining voluntary brotherhoods or guilds which took on many of the old functions of the family. Such a guild was established in Canterbury as early as the ninth century and later records prove the existence of guilds in several other English towns. A much larger body, the so-called "peace-guild" formed in London during the reign of Athelstan (924–939), enjoyed both church and royal support. Under the leadership of the bishops and officers of the crown, it attempted to check the crime which flourished around the country's greatest city. 93

Cnut (994–1035) turned every able-bodied male in the country into a policeman. All grown men were made to join a "tithing" of ten, each member of which was responsible for the good conduct of the others. So matters stood at the time of the Norman conquest of England.

Self-help with a water bucket was the only way of fighting fire in turbulent post-Roman Europe. Water pumps had disappeared along with the bands of trained firemen who had used them, and time after time the diminished towns which had ridden out the barbarian influx were devastated by flames. London, for instance, was almost completely destroyed in A.D. 798 and again in A.D. 982.

So many conflagrations started from domestic hearths left unattended at night that some rulers instituted the custom of curfew; the word comes from the French "couvre-feu" meaning "cover fire." On retiring to bed citizens were required to extinguish all lights and fires. The first English city known to have enforced this protective measure was Oxford, acting on the advice of Alfred the Great (848–899). After the Norman conquest the curfew became universal in England.

More than just a fire precaution, the curfew was also an extremely useful police regulation. Once it had been rung no one was allowed on the streets without good reason, so that criminals wishing to use the darkness to cloak their movements found it more difficult to escape detection. To ensure respect for the law from the ordinary people, the Normans continued with the tithing system which involved everybody except clergy or members of the nobility in the keeping of the king's peace.

Gradually the tithing method of policing fell into disuse, and new types of officials appeared. At the bottom of the scale was the constable, whose position had possibly evolved from that of the old tithing leaders, while above him, in towns big enough to need more than one policeman, came the beadle and the sergeants. In fourteenth-century London each ward of the city had a beadle who, besides directing the constables in their work of crime prevention, was also in charge of fire precautions. Beadle and constables settled brawls and minor crimes, but if things got out of hand and a real riot threatened, they sent for the sergeants. The sergeants, who came under the direct orders of the mayor of the town or the sheriff of the district, acted as a central reserve to deal with emergencies.

Despite the efforts of these medieval policemen violence was commonplace on the streets. These were days when most people carried at least a dagger, so that angry words often led to bloodshed. King Edward I's

Statute of Winchester of 1285 attempted to stamp out the prevalent lawlessness. It was made obligatory for all fit men to take part in the "hue and cry" after a wanted criminal, while to tighten up security at night the king ordered that every town should maintain a watch from sunset to sunrise.

Each citizen had reluctantly to take his turn at trudging through the darkened streets, but the job of the watch was at least made easier by the old custom of curfew, which kept decent people indoors after nightfall. Anyone whom the patrol met could be stopped for questioning, and arrested if his answers were not satisfactory.

The other function of the curfew was not forgotten. Fire remained a deadly enemy in a time when most buildings were still made of wood and thatch, and when bedding was often no more than a pile of straw. The watch kept an eye open for fires as well as felons, and made sure that all naked lights had been properly extinguished.

Cities also began to adopt other measures calculated to reduce the fire hazard. Under London's first Mayor, Henry FitzAlwin, a local law was passed in 1189 encouraging citizens to build in stone, and roof with tiles. FitzAlwin's recommendations went largely unheard. London had to learn the hard way. In 1212 an uncontrollable fire raged through its inflammable hovels, claiming three thousand lives. After that, roofs of rushes or thatch were outlawed from the capital. Walls, however, were a different matter. Few people could afford stone, so wood remained the predominant building material until the art of brick-making, lost to Europe since Roman times, was rediscovered in fourteenth-century Flanders.

Along with the slow spread of building restrictions came all sorts of other regulations. In the thirteenth century, London bakers were forbidden to burn straw or ferns to heat their ovens for fear the fire should flare up and get out of control. A century later Parisians were strictly forbidden to take a lantern into a stable. These rules were meant to stop fires starting at all; others were intended to provide the means of fighting fires once they had begun. During the fourteenth century both Paris and London demanded that each householder keep a tub of water in constant readiness by his door, while every London ward had to provide a strong iron hook for pulling down burning material.

Many cities devised alarm systems. In English towns it was generally the beadle's duty to summon aid to a blaze by blowing a horn, but Exeter appointed a special bellman in 1472 to warn its citizens of fire. The German cities of Merseburg and Leipzig posted fire watchers in high church towers to give instant notice of any outbreak. Such early warning was particularly necessary, for hooks and water buckets were feeble   95

An eighteenth-century London "Charlie" or watchman.

The Great Fire of London, 1666.

weapons against an established conflagration.

Judging from the account of Marco Polo, Chinese cities probably had better protection against both fire and crime than their European contemporaries. In his description of Hangchou, Marco mentions a patrol which roamed the streets by night to apprehend suspicious characters and to make sure that fires and lights had been put out at the appointed time. If the watchmen discovered an outbreak of fire they summoned assistance by banging a gong. Other guards, stationed on the numerous bridges which spanned the many channels of the city's river rushed up with water buckets at the ready. No ordinary citizen other than the actual householder was allowed to assist in extinguishing the flames because of the strictly enforced curfew. Marco estimated that Hangchou alone had between one and two thousand policemen cum firemen.

No comparable force existed in European cities for many a long year. In France after the English had finally been driven out at the end of the Hundred Years War, Charles VII (1403–61) did set up a sort of military police brigade to re-impose civil order, but the citizens' watch marching through the town streets remained the chief instrument for the suppression of crime after dark.

Though the system was showing signs of collapse, this was still largely true two centuries later when the British King, Charles II attempted to improve London's ramshackle law machine, which was more suited to a small country town than a roaring seventeenth-century metropolis. To replace the citizen "volunteers," one thousand paid watchmen, who were 97 afterwards contemptuously known as "Charlies," were recruited. Unfortunately the authorities could never attract the right sort of men. Most of the "Charlies" were either elderly or idle, and they quickly established a reputation for being anywhere other than the scene of a crime.

King Charles had other troubles. The Great Fire of London of 1666 occurred during his reign. Thirteen thousand houses were gutted leaving a hundred thousand people homeless, and further damage was prevented only because the monarch himself took personal charge, ordering houses to be blown up to make fire-breaks, and even passing fire buckets with his own hands.

After this catastrophe London's municipal authorities tightened up their fire regulations. The city was divided into four districts, each of which was to be supplied with eight hundred leather water buckets, fifty ladders of from 12 to 42 feet in length, and a number of pickaxes and shovels. In addition every parish was to have two large hand syringes or squirts. More important, however, the twelve main livery companies were each to provide, amongst other things, one of the hand-operated fire engines which had come into use in many German cities some fifty years before.

These early fire engines consisted of a pump and cistern mounted either on wheels or skids for rapid transit to the scene of a blaze. Water from the pump was directed onto the flames by a metal nozzle which could be swivelled to point in any direction. The cistern was kept filled with water by a chain of people passing buckets from hand to hand.

In 1673 Jan van der Heiden, who was the inspector of fire engines for the city of Amsterdam, made the first use of a flexible hose in fighting a fire. The leather hoses which he introduced enabled firemen to move in closer and direct a jet of water into the very heart of the blaze. Later he developed suction hoses up to a thousand feet long so that he was able to fill the cisterns of the fire engines without recourse to wasteful bucket chains.

Coupled with this advance in fire-fighting equipment came the gradual re-emergence of the trained fireman, whose trade had been forgotten since Roman times. Boston had a volunteer fire service in 1672, and by 1697 had become the first American town to pay its brigade. After 1708 each English parish was obliged to keep a large engine and a hand squirt in readiness, but unfortunately the efficiency of the volunteers who worked them was very much in doubt. Dickens has left a delightful account from a later date which illustrates the all too frequent bumbling. "Bang went the pumps, the people cheered, the beadle perspired profusely, but it was unfortunately discovered, just as they were going to put the fire out, that

Flexible hoses were first used at a fire in Amsterdam, 1673.

nobody understood the process by which the engine was filled with
water."

The Paris fire brigade was far better organized. Its beginning as a professional service may be traced back to 1699, when in exchange for a
trading monopoly granted by King Louis XIV the fire-engine manufacturer, M. Dumourrier Duperrier, agreed to provide a force of firemen from
amongst his own employees. Unlike their English counterparts the French-
men were experts, who thoroughly understood their pumps. Duperrier's 99

A mid-eighteenth century manual fire-engine in London.

brigade quickly established a reputation for efficiency, which it sustained under different leaders throughout the eighteenth century. In 1811 Napoleon reformed and expanded the Paris fire service to meet the increased demands of the fast-growing city. The brigade was put on a completely military footing with thirteen officers and 563 men.

The major British and American cities lagged far behind the French capital for many years. Although New York bought two English Newsham fire engines in 1731, recruited twenty-four volunteers to work the handles of the pumps in 1738, and thereafter slowly expanded its fire services, the city remained inadequately protected until the formation of the Metropolitan Fire Department in 1865. London was, if anything, even worse prepared. Until January 1866 the British capital, then a city of three million inhabitants, had virtually no public provision for fighting fire at all. Discounting the ineffectual parish engines, London's only protection was provided by the 130 full-time firemen and 40 part-timers employed by a consortium of fire insurance companies, which had merged their private brigades in 1833 to form the Fire Engine Establishment.

Many American cities in the nineteenth century relied completely on volunteer firemen, just as rural areas do today. In the 1860s Chicago, for instance, had over eight hundred firemen who gave up some of their leisure to protect their neighbours' property. Tragically, their efforts were unable to check the fire which swept through their town in 1871, killing 250 of the inhabitants, destroying over seventeen thousand buildings, and leaving a third of the area in ashes. Since that time fire-fighting in the great cities of the world has become more and more a highly professional and skilled undertaking.

Until the nineteenth century the policing of British and American towns
was, like their fire precautions, amateurish when compared with European

Refugees escaping across a bridge during the Great Fire of Chicago, 1871.

practice. In England the eighteenth century was the heyday for criminals. Each parish appointed one unpaid constable, who during his year of office was expected to keep peace in the neighbourhood singlehanded or, at most, with the help of a few decrepit "Charlies." As cities grew larger, making many fellow-townsmen complete strangers to one another, the constable's job became less and less enviable. Wealthier people started to pay substitutes to serve for them when their turn came round, and since

London's policemen in the mid-nineteenth century.

only a small fee was offered, fit and healthy men seldom applied for the position.

The early settlers in North America carried their English customs over the Atlantic to their new home. American towns were policed by parish constables, and just as in the homeland the system began to break down as townships developed into cities.

Behind the English-speaking people's reluctance to develop new ways of enforcing law in their cities, lay the deep rooted fear that an organized police force would undermine personal liberty. Rather than risk their freedom the British, like the Greeks before them, pinned their hopes on the deterrent power of a savage penal code, which by 1800 listed more than two hundred crimes punishable by death. London did have a small band of armed and uniformed "Runners," who from the middle of the eighteenth century worked under the orders of the Bow Street Court, but it was not until 1829 that the great capital, with even then well over a million inhabitants, grudgingly accepted a Metropolitan Police Force of two thousand men.

Organized police forces had a much earlier beginning on the Continent of Europe. The Prussian "Polizei-Ausreuter," established in 1719 by Friedrich Wilhelm I to "root out" crime, was perhaps the first modern 102 force, while by 1741 the policemen of Berlin had been placed under the

A New York policeman directing a stranger, 1898.

command of a single burgomaster, who acted as police chief. Paris was just as well served. According to Philip Thicknesse, an English visitor of 1767, the "interior police of Paris (were) very astonishing." He was so impressed by the number and vigilance of the guards that he felt it "next to an impossibility for a street-robber to escape with his booty."

After the War of Independence the American police system began to change. Parish constables were replaced by sheriffs elected in each county and marshalls elected in each town. As populations grew, the number of officers was increased, but each small force remained under the control of a locally elected sheriff or marshall. This tradition is still evident today. The 40,000 independent police forces, which protect modern American society, are an inefficient relic of the way law was kept in the past.

Modern police forces use sophisticated equipment like this helicopter flown by a New York City police officer.

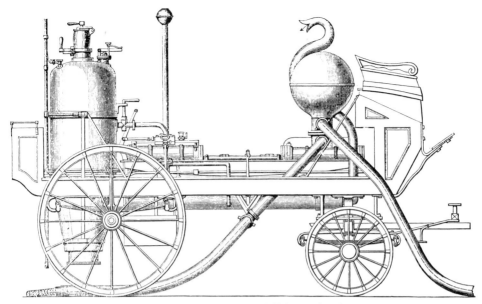
The first steam fire-engine made by Braithwaite and Ericsson in 1829.

Effective city police did not develop in the United States until well on in the nineteenth century. The almost complete lack of crime prevention machinery in even the old-established towns of the eastern seaboard can be judged from the stir caused in 1838 by Boston's decision to recruit six men to police its streets. It was not until New York instituted its eight-hundred-man force in 1844 that any American city could claim to be adequately protected against crime.

The present age of giant cities, anonymous populations and fast transport has made the criminal more elusive than ever before. Improved techniques are needed in the age-old battle to uphold the law. Cars, radio, photography, forensic science, and computer information banks have all become indispensable weapons in the police armoury. New duties have also come the policeman's way. Not only must crime be suppressed, but traffic must be controlled, parking laws enforced, crowds kept in order, and children helped across busy roads. Forces have expanded enormously since their early beginnings. The United States employs something like 300,000 policemen, while London which was so loath to accept any at all, now has about 20,000. Life in a modern city without a professional and highly trained police force would be unthinkable.

Today's firemen must be equally skilled to manage the powerful and complex appliances which have evolved from the feebler machines used by earlier brigades. The manual fire engines of the seventeenth and eighteenth centuries were relatively unsophisticated. Untrained men could be called out of the crowd, if need be, to take a turn on the pumping handles. Steam power gave fire-fighters a more effective tool, but made   105

The first petrol-driven fire-engine in public service, London 1904.

their trade more technical. The first steam fire engine appeared in 1830 and was built in England by the firm of Braithwaite and Ericsson. Only the pump was steam-operated. Horses still had to gallop the machine to the scene of the fire, but the steam power freed men from hand pumping and allowed them to concentrate on putting out the blaze. America's first steam fire engine, built in New York by Paul Hodge during the years 1840–41, had the added distinction of being the first self-propelled fire engine ever constructed. By the 1860s many United States' cities numbered a few steamers amongst their fire engines, while New York with its fleet of thirty-five horse-drawn steam pumps led the world.

The next major technical advance was the advent of the self-propelled petrol-driven fire engine in 1904. Finchley, in the suburbs of London, had the first of these vehicles to come into service with a public brigade. London saw the last of its steam fire engines in 1917, while New York's Fire Department became fully motorized in 1922. Nowadays cities the 106 world over are protected by self-propelled fire appliances, and petrol

Fire-fighting in modern New York.

engines have themselves given way to diesels.

Along with the technical progress came parallel advances in the size and efficiency of the fire brigades themselves, partly in response to city growth, but in some measure due to a demand for better protection. New York City will illustrate the point. In 1865 it employed just under fifteen hundred firemen to man its horse-drawn fire engines. The present force numbers something like twelve thousand and is equipped with powerful fire engines, extremely effective high pressure pumps, and mobile elevating platforms for rescue work. Towns are better protected than they have ever been, but there are new difficulties and problems. Buildings rise to unprecedented heights, while inflammable materials like petroleum are stored in great quantities. Fire is still a danger to be feared even in this modern world.

7

Work

The prosperity of the three great ancient civilizations, in Sumeria, Egypt, and the Indus Valley, rested squarely on irrigation agriculture. Even when cities developed, the majority of their citizens continued to labour on the land, though the increasing food surplus produced by more efficient farming techniques allowed a growing number to specialize in other crafts.

Sumerian texts mention some of the occupations which townsmen began to follow. Goldsmiths and jewellers were employed to fashion adornments for the rich, whose coiffures were carefully arranged by skilled hairdressers. Buildings were erected by specialized bricklayers, carpenters, and masons, and woe betide them if they did not know their job. According to the laws of Hammurabi if a house fell down and killed its owner, the builder was himself put to death. Spinners and weavers, using mainly wool in preference to the vegetable fibres favoured by their Egyptian contemporaries, worked to clothe their fellow citizens. The food trades were represented by bakers, brewers, butchers, and cooks, while fish must also have been sold since the existence of fresh- and salt-water fishermen is recorded. Smiths, working principally with bronze, were active in the manufacture of weapons and tools as well as luxury items like mirrors and bowls. Containers for everyday use were produced by potters and basket makers, the latter, in this land of reeds, being particularly adept in their calling.

Judging from the old biblical story of how the infant Moses floated safely down the Nile in a rush basket, the Egyptians must have shared this skill. Most of the jobs recorded in the Sumerian scripts must in fact have been paralleled in Egypt and along the Indus Valley. All three civilizations reached comparable levels of technological achievement. Craftsmen worked with the same materials and produced items intended for the same purposes, but distinct traditions of design developed in each culture. Potters, for instance, though all familiar with the use of the wheel, made pots which were easily recognizable as products of their own particular region.

In the course of time the number of townspeople engaged in agricultural 109

Ancient Egyptian craftsmen, part of a wall painting from the tomb of Nebamun, Thebes which dates from about 1400 B.C.

work began to dwindle. Specialization paid dividends in terms of improved techniques and new skills, so that home-made products could no longer compete with those of the artisan. The countryman was able to concentrate on farming, and look to the town for manufactured goods. Regular industries began to spring up. At the beginning of the second millennium B.C. nine thousand people were employed in and around Ur in manufacturing woollen textiles. Increasingly the city dweller's work as well as his environment separated him from the land which his ancestors had tilled.

Perhaps because the Greek city-state included a tract of farmland as well as an urban core, its townsmen never quite forgot that their roots were buried deep in their native soil. Even when a city waxed great as a centre of commerce and industry so that most of its citizens were engaged in completely urban crafts, there were always some who pursued agricultural callings. Many of the richer citizens divided their time between their city and farms or vineyards in the surrounding countryside. Athens, though the most industrialized city of its time, still retained close ties with the land. The countrymen of Attica had full rights as Athenian citizens and could make their voice heard in the city assembly.

Fifth century B.C. Athens was the first city to outgrow its local food supplies. It had to export manufactured goods or starve. High quality pots, bronzes, and furniture poured from its workshops to pay for Black Sea corn. Athenian merchant ships were busy throughout the Mediterranean. But commerce was only one side of the amazing variety of Athenian life. The city also excelled in the arts. Her sculptors reached new heights of

This fourth century B.C. Athenian crater has been decorated with scenes from the potter's workshop.

Chinese lacquerware of the Han dynasty.

perfection; her dramatists broke new ground; her philosophers made lasting contributions to human thought. Athens was one of the major landmarks in the progress of mankind.

Rome, though it eventually grew much larger than Athens, was never a truly industrial city. It lived on the tribute of its vast empire, and exported administrative skill rather than material objects. As a consequence the capital was plagued by a chronic unemployment problem which left many thousands dependent on the free corn dole to keep them from starvation. Many citizens did, however, lead a busy life, rising at dawn and putting in a good day's work before having the afternoon free for leisure.

The food and materials imported by the rapacious capital required the services of an army of dockers, lightermen, warehousemen, and carters. Other Romans were concerned with production. Local market gardener brought their own vegetables and flowers into the city for sale. Brick kilns smoked busily just outside the walls, while within the confines of the city ropemakers, leather tanners, and metal workers carried on their various trades. Many shopkeepers made what they sold. The shoe seller's merchandise was made on the premises; so was the clothier's. Goldsmiths, jewellers, and ivory carvers busy over their precious wares were always ready to break off and haggle with a customer. The producing and manufacturing industries were, however, nearly all small-scale enterprises aimed at satisfying a purely local demand.

Han China, which flourished at about the same time as the Roman Empire, did, on the other hand, maintain large government-operated factories although its economy was basically agricultural. In the middle of the last century B.C. the state workshops in the textile towns of eastern China employed several thousand operatives to turn out silks for the rich, and rough hempen cloth for the poor.

Other Han towns were devoted to the state iron industry. Foundries were built at pit-heads, so that iron could be mined, smelted, and worked in the same location. Bronze was gradually being relegated to decorative uses, and the iron factories were kept busy making swords and spearheads for the army as well as ploughshares and hoes for the farmers.

Another important urban industry in China was the production of lacquer ware. The government had a finger in this pie too, and at the beginning of the Christian era there were several state workshops supplementing the output of numerous private concerns. All manner of objects, ranging from small bowls, dishes, and cups to such large items as coffins, were lacquered with juice extracted from the lac tree. The cheapest lacquer ware was shaped out of wood, but a really delicate piece might owe its form to nothing more than a piece of hempen cloth, cunningly modelled and stiffened with successive layers of varnish.

Silks and lacquers were still much in demand when the thirteenth-century Venetian traveller Marco Polo visited China, a thousand years after the fall of the Han dynasty. The country had recently suffered invasion and lay beneath the heel of the alien Mongols, but despite the destruction of war the number and prosperity of the cities were enough to amaze the western visitor. Kinsai was the greatest wonder of all with, allegedly, 144,000 workshops employing between ten and forty men apiece. The figures are obviously exaggerated, but Kinsai must have been a considerable manufacturing centre, and it by no means stood alone. Time and again Marco mentioned cities which lived by "trade and industry" and had "silk in plenty." Some industries, in their infancy in the Han era, had risen to new prominence. The manufacture of gilded cloth was carried on in many towns, and porcelain had come much into favour, though according to Marco its production was confined to only one city.

Medieval Europe could not rival the commercial activity of the Chinese. The Western World was still recuperating from the ills inflicted on it by the fall of Rome. Town life had begun to flourish again in the eleventh century, but right until the end of the Middle Ages most European cities were small by Chinese standards.

Small though they were, these budding towns became centres of industry for the surrounding country districts. The weekly market attracted enough customers to encourage the townsmen to concentrate on specialist crafts and to leave serious agriculture to the farmers. Not that the city-dwellers cut themselves off completely from the land. They lived too near it for that. Most worked a garden plot and continued to keep pigs and cattle which spent their nights in town and their days grazing the common pasturage outside the walls. When harvest time came around there was in some towns a mass exodus into the country to help carry in the crops. It is recorded that during the thirteenth century work on building the town wall of Coblenz in Germany had to be temporarily suspended because all the citizens had gone harvesting.

For most of the year, however, the townsman was mainly concerned with working at his trade. Nearly everyone made, or at least modified, what he sold. There were few who simply retailed for a living. Butchers had to slaughter the beasts as well as bring the carcasses and hides into market for sale. Animal skins were a very important item in medieval commerce and many markets made it a rule that butchers could only retail meat if they brought the hides with them for sale to the local tanners and tawers.

These were two distinct groups of tradesmen, which were strictly forbidden to meddle in one another's business. Tanners converted ox, cow, and calf hides into leather by allowing them to lie for up to a year in a liquor extracted from boiled oak bark. Tawers cured sheep, deer, and horse skins by the quicker process of steeping them in a solution of alum and then rubbing them with oil.

There was never any shortage of buyers for leather. The tanned variety was needed by shoemakers, saddlers, harness makers, and bottle makers, while the softer product of tawing was much in demand for gloves, purses, and parchment. The strength of the medieval leather industry may be judged from the fact that of the two thousand people who lived in fourteenth-century Oxford getting on for fifty were engaged in some aspect

Medieval dyers at work. Trades such as this were controlled by craft guilds.

of the trade.

Bakers and brewers were also very numerous. Few of the poorer people had ovens at home, and bakers quite often not only made bread but also cooked the pies and pasties brought to them by their patrons. In England ale was the universal beverage, and great quantities were brewed. Many women prepared ale for family consumption, and some became so skilful that they set up as ale-wives and catered for others. If the figures available for the little Kentish town of Faversham are typical, then an almost incredible number of townswomen must have become involved in the business. When Faversham's traders were assessed for a special tax in 1327, no less than 84 of the 250 who had to pay were ale-wives.

Although far fewer in number than the brewers, some blacksmiths, masons, and carpenters could be found in every town. Other trades were less widespread. Gold- and coppersmiths were more likely to set up shop in the larger cities, while clothmaking and its associated skills were characteristic of relatively few centres, though practised on a small scale in many towns.

Whatever trade the late medieval townsman followed, it was controlled by a craft guild. Originally each town had only one commercial guild, which protected its own craftsmen by levying a toll on all outsiders who came to sell at the local market. Separate craft guilds emerged later as communities grew large enough to support several people working at the same trade. This splitting up process made a start in the twelfth century, and by the middle of the thirteenth most municipalities had their guilds of tanners, tawers, butchers, bakers, and all the rest.

The guilds performed a number of socially useful functions. They protected the consumer by insisting on high standards of workmanship. A member found guilty of sharp practice was fined, and repeated transgressions resulted in his expulsion from the guild and exclusion from the town market. Under the guild system young people could receive a vocational training. Master craftsmen took on apprentices and in return for several years of unpaid work taught them a trade. At the end of their apprenticeships, the newly fledged artisans became journeymen who could demand wages in return for their labours. In the course of time an ambitious journeyman could submit a sample of his work to the guild, and if this masterpiece was acceptable he was then free to set up as an independent master craftsman on his own.

Craft guilds reached the peak of their power during the thirteenth and fourteenth centuries. Subsequently deficiencies in their organization became more apparent, and their faults began to outweigh their merits. 115

One trouble was that guilds were founded on a town basis, and not designed to promote the freer flow of trade demanded by Europe's expanding economy. Another difficulty was the narrow self-interest of some guild leaders, who sought to protect themselves from competition by blocking the efforts of promising journeymen to gain master status. The gap between established masters and their workers began to widen, and guild unity suffered. Journeymen started to form themselves into separate guilds which would look after their interests instead of those of the masters.

The craft guilds were also undermined by separatist movements amongst the employers, some of whom had found it more profitable to retail than to manufacture. Such traders broke away from the old craft guilds and founded companies whose membership was confined to retailers. London had well-established livery companies like the Grocers and Merchant Taylors in the fourteenth century, and similar bodies were formed in the provincial cities during the following hundred years.

Merchants specializing in buying and selling had no scruples about breaking through the monopolies exercised by craft guilds. Wool merchants in particular took business away from townsmen by encouraging the peasants who had previously supplied the raw wool to work it into yarn and cloth themselves.

Although craft guilds lost their absolute control of industry their decline was very gradual. Rich merchants might dominate the market, but throughout the sixteenth and seventeenth centuries and even into the eighteenth the master craftsmen of each city regulated the entry of apprentices to their trade and decided which journeymen were fit to be included in their number.

The old tradition of apprenticeship was still sufficiently strong to spread across the sea to Colonial America. Young Americans in the seventeenth and eighteenth centuries accepted it as natural that they should be placed with a master to learn a trade. Skill accumulated from generation to generation, and some cities began to build up substantial reputations in particular crafts. Early eighteenth-century Boston was noted for its silverware, and Philadelphia was a centre for furniture making.

But developments in Britain were about to change the whole way in which industry was managed. Self-employed men had been growing steadily fewer since medieval time. Adam Smith, the economist, estimated in his *Wealth of Nations*, written in 1776, that only one man in twenty was his own master. Manufacturing concerns were, however, for the most part still small enough for the employer to know all his workers as individuals.

116 The Industrial Revolution bursting on Britain in the last quarter of the

Early nineteenth-century factory children.

eighteenth century accelerated the movement away from self-employment, and created a factory system in which people felt mere cogs in a machine. Steam- and water-power gave the manufacturer the means of mass-production and, as one contemporary writer stated, "men, women, and children [were] yoked together with iron and steam."

People attracted into towns by the higher wages which could be earned in mushrooming factories found the gains illusory. Traditional freedoms were eroded. A lament published in the trade union magazine *Pioneer* of 19 October 1833 expressed some of the bitterness of a cruelly exploited generation: "The green grass and the healthful hayfield are shut out from our path. The whistling of birds is not for us — our melody is the deafening noise of the engine. The merry fiddle and the humble dance will send us to the treadmill. We eat the worst food, drink the worst drink — our raiments, our houses, our everything, bear signs of poverty, and we are gravely told that this must be our lot."

Tiny children as well as men and women were caught up in the pitiless system and made to toil for long hours at repetitive tasks. Child labour was no new thing, but where before it had been within a family environment it was now in a vast, impersonal setting. Children of as little as five years old went to work in the dark and came home often just in time to be put straight to bed.

Townspeople had rarely been subject to such widespread oppression as were the British factory operatives of the early nineteenth century. Unrest was rife when, perhaps just in time to prevent major disturbances, the government moved to eradicate some of the worst abuses. It was the children whom Parliament sought to protect. The Factory Act of 1833 forbad the employment of any child under nine years of age and ruled that even those eligible for work should do no more than forty-eight hours in a week. A great step forward was the recruitment of a factory inspectorate to ensure that the Act was obeyed. Conditions improved still further with the adoption of the Ten Hour Bill of 1847 which limited the daily working time for women and youths to ten hours. In the textile mills so many of the employees were women and children that once they had gone home all the machinery had to be shut down. There was nothing for it but to reduce the men's hours as well.

Enlightened measures from above were matched by determined pressure from below. Britain was the pioneer of the trade union movement. Late in the eighteenth century some of the new industrial workers conceived the idea of banding together to strengthen their bargaining power. These

early efforts were quickly squashed. With the example of the overthrown

Mass production techniques provide the amenities of modern life only by reducing traditional pride in labour.

French monarchy across the Channel the ruling classes were in no mood for concessions, and saw the seeds of rebellion in any association of working-men. Trade unions were made illegal in England by the Combination Laws of 1799 and 1800, which stayed in force until 1824. After that time unions made more progress though the opposition remained strong. Many employers refused to negotiate with them, while strikers were likely to find themselves classed as vagrants by the magistrates and to be thrown into prison. By the middle of the nineteenth century, however, many of the craftsmen had won recognition for their unions, but another fifty years had to pass before the less skilled workers achieved a similar success.

Office workers crowding into New York City.

Since those early days of British industrialization many nations have trod the same path, and workers in factory towns all over the world have faced the same battles. Trade unions have become an accepted feature in the economic life of all industrial countries, and have helped gain for their members a fairer share of the benefits of mass production.

Technology has created new forms of power, new materials, and new industries. Water and steam have given way to electricity; iron has been replaced by steel and plastics; natural textile fibres have been largely crowded out by synthetic products. Cars, aeroplanes, domestic appliances, electronic devices — all undreamt of a hundred years ago — pour from the factories. The armies of office workers who throng daily into the great cities are needed to control and facilitate the vast flow of trade. There are more products, more luxuries, and more varieties of employment than ever before, but many feel alienated from an impersonal society. A great deal was lost as well as gained when factory methods ousted the small workshop. The comforts of the industrial city cannot fully recompense those who feel deprived of a pride in their work and a respected place in the community.

8

Buying and Selling

A city with its multitude of potential customers is a natural focus for buying and selling. Craftsmen will set up business within its sheltering walls; local countrymen will be attracted to barter their surplus food for manufactured goods; merchants will bring in luxuries and raw materials from more distant places to exchange for the town's own products. It was no accident that the Hittites, an early Middle Eastern race of city builders, derived their words for "market" and "town" from a common root. Town and market go together.

Yet strangely enough the very first cities seem to have been exceptions to the rule. The larger urban households in Sumeria were nearly self-supporting, growing their own food in fields outside the walls and setting their slaves to make clothes, plait baskets, and even manufacture pots. Those citizens who were servants of palace or temple were supported by grants of food and other necessaries from the royal or priestly store-rooms. There was little need for trade between fellow townsmen, and as far as is known no special area was set aside for buying and selling in early Sumerian cities. Not until the second millennium B.C. is there even any mention of the small shop in which a craftsman might sell his wares.

Sumeria's commercial energies, thwarted at home, were turned outwards and concentrated on foreign trade. The country's only natural assets were the mud and reeds from which its cities were largely built. Every piece of stone or wood needed to construct a palace or temple, every lump of precious metal, every gem had to be imported. The Sumerians had a surplus of textiles and barley which they used to pay for their imports. Early Sumerian cities might have lacked market stalls and the cries of competing vendors, but the quays of their riverside harbours were clamorous with the haggling of merchants and the comings and goings of ships from far away places.

By late in the third millennium B.C. some vessels even came across the Arabian Sea and up the Persian Gulf from towns which were springing   121 up along the River Indus. These cities were organized very differently from those of Sumer. There were no temple workshops nor, with the exception of the municipal granaries, any centralized warehouses from which workers could be paid in commodities. Craftsmen like potters and smiths seem to have always been free to sell their products direct to the public, so that each artisan's premises became a shop. The straight, nine-hundred-yard sweep of Mohenjo-daro's main thoroughfare was enlivened at intervals by such craftsmen's workshops where goods were both manufactured and laid out for sale. One large building with circular depressions in its floor to support wine jars was probably a restaurant, but in that age before coined money it is something of a mystery how the customers paid their bills.

Shopping in Egypt was also complicated by a general lack of easily portable wealth. Barter remained the chief mode of trade long after it became customary under the New Kingdom (sixteenth to eighth century B.C.) to price articles at so many uten or spirals of copper wire. Most people were still paid for their labours in kind, and went to the town market to swop rather than to buy.

The Greek historian Herodotus, whose fellow countrymen of the fifth century B.C. produced some of the world's most beautiful coins, credited the Lydians of Asia Minor with the actual invention of money. Money was a great step forward in the history of shopping, and eased the problems of marketing enormously. It was no longer necessary to barter or weigh out great chunks of metal. A universally acceptable purchasing power could be carried in the pocket.

At the heart of each Greek city lay its agora, a central open space into which was focussed all the restless energy of the community. There was always something to attract a crowd. If not the market stalls it might be a new teacher from abroad, a public meeting, some kind of theatrical show, or even a religious festival. As a city advanced in population and wealth the simple open space gave way to a grander agora flanked by colonnaded buildings which sheltered rows of shops and offices.

Excavations along the north side of the agora at Corinth have revealed a covered fishmarket dating from the fifth century B.C. Each shop had a water-tight tank in which fish were kept alive until selected by a customer. Most foodstuffs were still sold, however, from temporary booths put up in the agora. Athens' open market continued to thrive even when the great Stoa of Attalus, over one hundred yards long and two storeys high, gave the city an extra forty-two elegant shops during the second century B.C.

Like the Greek agora, the Roman forum was more than a mere market.

A reconstruction of Trajan's Forum in Rome showing the multi-storey market building in the background.

It was the political as well as the commercial centre of the city. The original Forum in Rome developed in a marshy valley which, unlike the firmer ground of the surrounding seven hills, had remained uncluttered with buildings. Here was the natural meeting place where citizens gathered to exchange goods and gossip and to debate public affairs.

As Rome's population and power increased the city outgrew its ancient Forum, and new market squares were added by the emperors Julius Caesar, Augustus, and Trajan. Trajan's Forum, built early in the second century A.D., was the largest and most impressive of all with one side dominated by a five-storey market building containing 150 shops. Oil, wine, and spice merchants occupied the lower storeys of this massive structure, while the top floor was given over to a fishmarket where live fish were kept in both fresh- and salt-water pools.

But even with this mighty concentration of commerce there was still plenty of custom for traders who set up business in streets away from the Forum. The ground-floor rooms of many insulae were built with wide, arched doorways giving access to the street, so that each apartment could be let out as a shop. During the day the shop door stood open to display the goods for sale, but at nightfall the store-keeper protected his stock by pulling a folding wooden shutter across the gap and locking up securely.

Rome was a magnet not only for all that her own vast empire could produce, but also for luxury goods from lands outside her boundaries. 123

A Roman butcher's shop.

Silks filtered in from China, costly spices were imported from India, while from the imperial domains poured in building stone, bricks and timber, corn, meat, fruit, wines and cooking oils, metals, ivory, and glass. The Roman consumers could choose from the best available in the whole world.

Compared with the plenty and variety of Rome, European medieval cities were very poor places. International trade had collapsed with the fall of the Roman Empire, and was slow to revive. The towns of the early Middle Ages served as purely local market outlets. Peasants from the surrounding countryside brought in their surplus food, and hoarded the money they earned to pay their taxes or to purchase from the town craftsmen the few things they could not make for themselves. Manufactured goods were in such short supply that a length of cloth was a prized possession, and a sword a valued heirloom.

In an age of low populations it was to everyone's advantage for a special day to be set aside for marketing so that buyers and sellers could be sure of meeting. Canterbury held regular markets as early as the eighth century, and during the next two hundred years similar practices grew up in many European towns. The earliest markets were often held on Sundays when people from outlying districts came into town to worship and stayed on to buy. After-service markets were common in England under the Saxon kings, and despite the Church's objections were not finally suppressed until the thirteenth century.

A market stall outside a medieval town gate, an illustration from a mid-fifteenth century manuscript.

As markets became firmly established, they gradually hedged themselves about by all manner of rules. Some were intended to protect the consumer. Bread and ale, the basic necessities of life in medieval times, were kept as cheap as possible. In the absence of small denomination coins the price of a loaf of bread or a gallon of ale could not easily be altered, but the weight or strength could be, and was, controlled by town officials. When grain was plentiful and least expensive, loaves had to be heavier and ale less diluted. The reverse was true in times of scarcity. Brewers and bakers were allowed only a slender margin of profit.

The cornering and subsequent resale of goods at artificially high prices 125 was also prevented. Selling before the market opened, usually at about six o'clock in the morning, was strictly forbidden, and during the first few hours of trading only private individuals could buy. The demands of ordinary people were satisfied before bulk buyers were allowed into the market to purchase what was left. Beverley in Yorkshire was particularly severe in making its bakers wait until one o'clock to buy their corn, but more moderate rules of the same sort applied in other English cities. No large scale transactions in food were countenanced in the market at York until ten o'clock, while London's fishmongers had to wait for mass to finish at certain named churches before rushing off to buy fish to retail to the public.

Other rules looked after the interests of the traders. In medieval cities resident stallkeepers expected preferential treatment. Tolls were exacted from "foreign" merchants at the town gates, and admission was only granted after the peak selling period had passed. Local men always secured the best places for their stalls, and "foreigners" usually found themselves restricted to the quietest part of the market.

Traders groaned at the tolls, but still they came with their goods because opportunities to sell were so limited. Even towards the end of the medieval period towns which held more than one market a week were few and far between, and in the whole of England London was the only city where stalls were pitched on every day except Sunday. A provincial townsman who wanted steady sales had to go the rounds of neighbouring communities, and pay whatever tolls were demanded.

Although market day remained the great trading occasion of the week when crowds rolled in and every citizen with anything to sell set up a stall in the street, customers knew that at other times they could find the craftsman in his workshop. Casual sales out of market hours encouraged some tradesmen to convert their homes into shops. Only slight structural alterations were needed. Street doors were widened and fitted with wooden shutters which could be folded outwards to make a counter. By the early fourteenth century London contained enough of these shops for their intrusions into the highways to become a serious nuisance. A law had to be passed during the reign of Edward II limiting the width of shop counters in the capital to $2\frac{1}{2}$ feet, while a similar regulation enacted in Coventry stipulated that no counter should jut out beyond the house eaves. Shops were becoming commonplace, but not all tradesmen were at first allowed the privilege of selling from them. London's bakers were compelled to bring all their bread into the market place until the law was relaxed in

1302. Even where there was no legal compulsion many people preferred to sell from a stall, and right through the Middle Ages most food commodities were bought and sold in the open air.

The opening up of the world by exploration during the fifteenth and sixteenth centuries began to put new products into the shops, while the flood of treasure carried back to Europe from overseas conquests put more money into circulation. Demand and supply both increased.

One of the most noticeable changes in the pattern of urban trading during the sixteenth and seventeenth centuries was the appearance of much larger numbers of shops which retailed what other people had made. Some craftsmen with particularly flourishing shops found themselves unable to produce enough to keep up with demand. Such men began to buy goods from poorer colleagues for subsequent resale, and gradually gave less of their time to producing and more to selling. Shop and workshop were finally parting company.

Shop design was also changing. By the close of the seventeenth century the old folding leaves which let down into the street were fast being replaced by glass windows and indoor counters. Better-class customers expected to come inside to make their purchases, although poorer people remained content to buy across an open sill for another hundred years.

Early shop windows were made up of small panes of bottle glass. These let in the light and kept out the weather, but because of their distorting properties did little to encourage the display of goods. It was only after about 1750, when plate glass came more into vogue, that shopkeepers found it worthwhile to mount attractive exhibitions in their windows.

Despite other changes selling techniques were slow to alter. Both customer and salesman still accepted the time-honoured practice of haggling over the price, while shopkeepers were nearly always willing to extend credit in order to clinch a deal. Debts sometimes dragged on for months before they were settled, so to stay in business a trader had to allow himself a very handsome profit margin.

About 1780 a haberdasher's on London Bridge, Flint and Palmer's, invented a new way of selling which eventually revolutionized the retail trade. The profit per item was drastically reduced, but prices were fixed and absolutely no credit was granted. Although some customers were offended and bought elsewhere, the lure of cheaper goods won the day, and the business thrived. No time was lost arguing over prices, sales were brisk, and ready cash rather than promises rolled in. Lackington, the London bookseller, made a fortune by adopting the same system a few years later, but fixed price shops were considered a little undignified and remained a rarity until well on into the nineteenth century.

A seventeenth-century shopping street.

Along with the wrangling over prices other old-fashioned customs persisted. It was still common for slum dwellers without an oven of their own to prepare their Sunday meal at home and take it to the baker's for cooking. Wages were low, and many families haunted the pawnshops, pledging their meagre possessions to secure a few extra coppers. Such people were forced by their circumstances to patronize the general stores or chandlers' where prices were inflated, but where even the poor could obtain credit.

Even the great changes in society, which took place as industrialization gathered pace during the first part of the nineteenth century, did little to shake the retail trades out of their traditional ways. Most food still came from local farms, and was sold from market stalls or from the barrows of the hawkers who visited the outlying streets of the expanding towns. Other goods were bought in leisurely fashion. The customer sat down while the shopkeeper brought out articles for inspection. Prices were seldom fixed so bargaining prolonged nearly every sale. Chain stores were unknown, and most shops were operated in person by the owner.

Tailors and shoemakers continued to manufacture on their premises, although the mass production of cheap garments was just beginning, while a really medieval touch was provided by the milk shops which kept a cow

or two in their back rooms. London had seven hundred such establishments as late as the 1880s before the railways finally put them out of business by bringing in fresh milk from outlying areas. For many years the only noticeable change brought by the new technology was in the duration of the working day. Gas lights enabled shopkeepers to extend their hours of business until their wretched assistants were expected to work through to ten o'clock on weekdays and up to midnight on Saturdays.

After the mid-nineteenth century, however, major alterations began to undermine the accepted pattern of retailing, and the modern age of shopping dawned. English co-operative stores, which had been founded in the 1840s, discovered during the next decade that it was profitable to open branches. The idea of chain stores was introduced, and the old predominance of the owner shopkeeper began to wane. In the 1870s grocery chain stores opened up all over Britain to cater for the needs of a working class whose numbers made up for what its members lacked in individual wealth. Cheap food was imported from abroad, and all sorts of unaccustomed luxuries brought within reach of ordinary people. The grocery chains were followed in the 1880s by multiple tailors', chemists', and shoe shops with branches in most important towns.

Chain stores were a British innovation, but France was the home of the

Old and new shop fronts in eighteenth-century London

department store, now such a feature of city centres. The first department store was the Bon Marché, whose success with the Parisian public in the 1860s encouraged similar ventures in many Western cities. Large general shops, which over the years had been slowly widening their stock, took the plunge and blossomed into department stores. Stewart's, and Lord and Taylor's in New York were amongst the first old-established firms to transform themselves, while new concerns appeared aiming at department store status from the beginning. Marshall Field's of Chicago, founded in 1865, was one of the latter. Today, even though department stores have probably passed their peak of popularity, there is scarcely a major city in the world without its share of these giant shops.

In the twentieth century the United States has been the pace-maker in altering retail practices. Supermarkets began during the depression years of the 1930s. A wide variety of food products was displayed on open racks and customers served themselves. Price reductions quickly reconciled the public to the loss of personal service, and before long people dis-

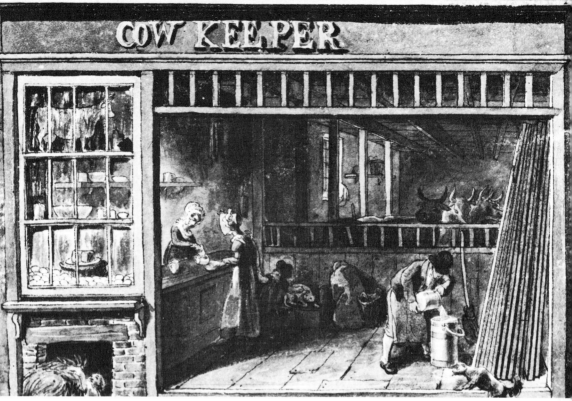

An early nineteenth-century London milk shop.

The bargain counter in a late nineteenth-century New York department store.

Extensive parking lots around a modern American suburban shopping centre.

covered a new pleasure in browsing amongst the shelves. Since the Second World War the idea of supermarkets has been taken up enthusiastically by the rest of the Western world, so that the old-style grocer's shop is fast fading from the city scene.

Other American innovations have as yet had less impact abroad. Discount houses became important in the 1950s by applying supermarket methods to the sphere of consumer goods sales. By curtailing service the discount houses were able to offer electrical appliances, home furnishings, and electronic equipment at prices far below those possible in conventional shops.

Another major change in the pattern of American retailing has been the development of suburban shopping centres tailor-made for the automobile era. In the last two decades new shopping areas featuring ample car parking space have sprung up on the outskirts of most large United States towns. With the increasing use of motor cars this practice is likely to spread to most cities of the world.

Over the centuries shops have slowly altered to suit the tastes and material resources of their age. In the last hundred years changes have been more rapid than ever before, and undoubtedly shops of the future will be very different from those of the present. But whatever progress brings, cities will remain, as they have nearly always been, places where things are bought and sold.

9
Pleasure and Leisure

Men have always needed some relaxation from the everyday business of life. Even the most primitive tribes had their legends and games, and with the advent of cities came the possibility of more sophisticated, and sometimes more depraved, pleasures.

Little is known about the leisure activities of the ordinary Sumerians, who lived in the world's first cities. Texts of the period mainly record the routine doings of the kings and the financial transactions of the temples, while even the few legends, which survive to show that stories were

Ancient Egyptian musicians, part of a wall-painting from the tomb of Nebamun dating from 1400 B.C.

Wrestling was a favourite sport of the Greek city dwellers.

appreciated, are mostly concerned with the ruling class. Probably religious ceremonies were both a source of spiritual well-being and the main form of entertainment. Singing and dancing featured in the festivals of the city gods, and sometimes legends were re-enacted before the congregation. A favourite secular pastime was wrestling, which was mentioned in the ancient legend of Gilgamesh and depicted in at least one lively group of statuettes.

The pleasures of the parallel civilization of Egypt were very similar. Wrestling was popular with the young men, and dancing and music appealed to everyone. Noblemen maintained their own private orchestras, but even the common people had their chance to thrill to the sound of drums, tambourines, strings, woodwinds, and brass as the musicians paraded through the streets on holy days. Acrobats provided another enjoyment, while in their quieter moments the Egyptians played a board game controlled by the throwing of dice.

Sinister rumours about the bulls of Minos must have been carried to Egypt aboard trading vessels from the maritime cities of Crete. Bull-jumping was the most popular of Cretan sports, at least with the spectators. A young man or girl stood in front of a ferocious bull, challenging it until it charged. An instant before the infuriated beast could strike home, the performer would seize its lowered horns, somersault onto its back and, if successful, jump unharmed to the ground. Many did not succeed. However, there was a gentler side to Minoan town life. The religious festivals were full of music and dancing. According to Homer's description in the *Iliad*, the young men and maidens formed a human chain before whirling madly round in a circle to the music of double pipe and harp. Dancing held such sway over the island people that the later Greeks became convinced that the art was a Cretan discovery.

Even in 1100 B.C. at about the time they destroyed the power of Minos, the Greeks had a strongly developed interest in athletics. Archaeological

Theatre of Dionysus in Athens.

The Theatre of Pompey, Rome's oldest and largest theatre, with the awning spread.

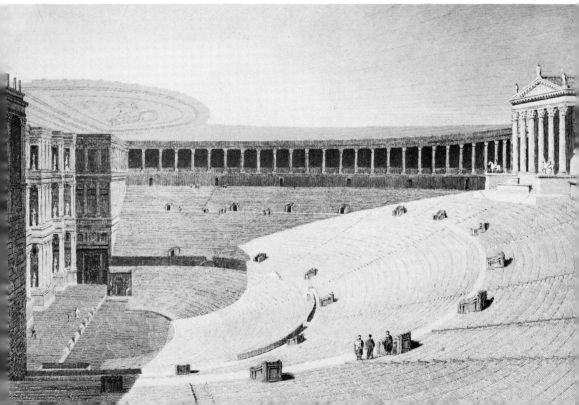

evidence suggests that already, at this early date, games were regularly held at Olympia. After a long gap, these contests were revived in 776 B.C., and from then until A.D. 392 Olympic Games were held every four years. Originally there was only one race, but gradually more competitions were added. Nearly every city in the Hellenic world sent representatives, and most young Greeks dreamt of Olympic honours. All Greek towns of any size boasted a gymnasium, where the men gathered for athletic training. The earliest gymnasiums were rather like modern sports grounds. They had dressing rooms and baths, running tracks, and open space for ball games, wrestling, and riding. Later on, by about the fourth century B.C., the layout became more formal with rooms clustered around a colonnaded courtyard. Often the gymnasium was associated with an open-air stadium where citizens could watch their champions race. Wherever possible the Greeks used the natural lie of the land to build much of their stadium for them. The track was placed at the base of a slope, which was dug away to give a terrace for spectators. Earth from the excavation was piled up on the other side of the arena to provide further seating.

Although devoted to athletics, the Greek city-dwellers did not spend all their leisure time in physical exercise. They accorded equal value to things of the mind. It was the Greeks who gave city life one of its major intellectual pleasures – the theatre.

Greek theatre is thought to have developed out of an act of worship. It was the custom in Athens for a chorus of fifty men to sing in praise of the wine god, Dionysus. In the course of time songs about other gods were included, and legends were recited. The audience came as much to hear the programme as out of religious duty. By the sixth century B.C. Athens had a rudimentary open-air theatre near the base of the Acropolis hill. The performers moved within a circle of flattened ground, while above them the spectators sat on the slope of the hillside, possibly on benches but quite probably on the bare earth. It was in this theatre that Thespis won the world's first dramatic prize, and so gave his name to the whole acting profession.

A century later when the plays of the first great dramatist, Aeschylus, were acted out, the natural site had long been modified and improved. The slope of the hillside had been steepened and low stone seats had been set into the ground. Those of the audience who wanted comfort had, however, to bring their own cushions to the show.

By the fourth century B.C. a love for the drama had spread throughout the Greek world, and no self-respecting city could afford to be without a theatre. Unfortunately the early flowering of theatrical art had already

136

spent itself. There were few playwrights of note, and light comedy was replacing soul-searching tragedy.

The Romans imported much of Greek theatre design into Italy, but made some important changes. Instead of using an excavated hillside, the Romans built up masonry to support the tiers of seats. Further, they employed a high stage reminiscent of the platforms used for the native mime plays of Italy rather than the Greek theatre's simple circle of beaten earth.

Most big towns in the Roman Empire came to possess a theatre of imposing proportions. Rome itself had three, and the oldest, built in 55 B.C., could seat 27,000 people. This huge size could be achieved because the building had no roof, although audiences could be protected from the sun by awnings spread out on hot days. A modern touch was supplied by curtains, which could be drawn across the stage at the end of an act.

Despite the magnificence of Roman theatres they housed a debased and dying art. The Roman public demanded spectacle, and the very size of the auditorium precluded any subtlety of acting. Serious plays were ousted by tasteless musical shows and obscene mimes. Cruelty and sensation were exploited to the full, but perhaps the theatre reached its lowest point in the reign of Domitian (A.D. 81–96), when, in the pursuit of realism, the emperor allowed a criminal to be tortured to death on the stage.

For all its pandering to popular taste the Roman theatre could never rival chariot racing and gladiatorial shows in the affections of the people. By the first century A.D., during the reign of Claudius, Rome enjoyed 159 holidays, and on 93 of them the state provided some kind of free entertainment. The emperors sought to keep ordinary men's minds off politics by sating them with blood and spectacle.

Rome's first track for chariot racing, the Circus Maximus, lay at the bottom of a valley whose slopes seated the watchers. Gradually the natural site was modified. Permanent stables were installed in 329 B.C., and in 189 B.C. the central earth bank, the so-called spine around which the chariots circled, was decorated with fine statues of the gods. In 46 B.C. Julius Caesar threw a moat about the whole area, and ordered the hillsides to be steepened to allow room for more spectators. By the beginning of the second century A.D. the steep banks of the stadium could hold up to 150,000 screaming fans.

A day at the races offered the ordinary Roman nearly all his heart desired. There was the beauty of the horses and their equipment, the bravery of the charioteers, the excitement and danger of the races, and the

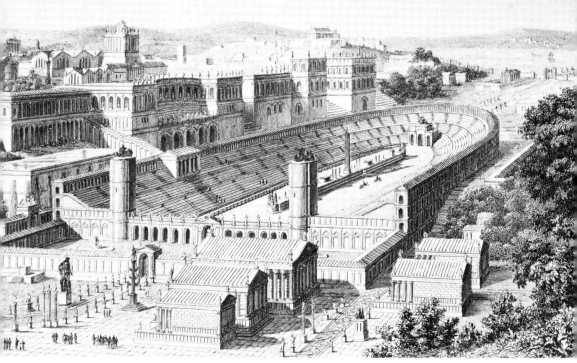

Reconstruction of the Circus Maximus at Rome.

opportunity of betting. All this could be enjoyed in a magnificent setting often in company with the Emperor himself. And there was no entry fee.

Tension would mount as preparations were made behind the scenes. While the crowd rehearsed the betting odds, the teams of four horses were harnessed up. Then the charioteers stepped into their vehicles, wound the reins around their bodies, adjusted their leather crash helmets, and waited. A trumpet rang out summoning the chariots into the starting stalls. The whole vast stadium fell silent as the sponsor of the games rose in his box and threw down the white handkerchief which signalled the start. Instantly the doors of the stalls flew open and the chariots flashed into sight to the accompaniment of a great roar from the spectators.

At the very beginning of the race the charioteer faced an awkward choice. Should he go flat out to gain the favoured station against the spine, or should he hang back? Two hundred yards from the gates an ominous white rope stretched tautly across the track. If the judges deemed the start to have been fair the rope would drop, but many luckless teams came to grief when the rope stayed put.

There were other hazards. A miscalculated turn could easily smash a
flimsy chariot against the spine and pitch the driver headlong into the

path of a rival team. Even if the thrown man were lucky enough to escape the trampling hooves he still had to extricate himself from the reins to avoid being dragged to death by his own horses. Most charioteers carried a dagger to cut themselves free. Foul play was not unknown. A favourite trick was to jerk off an opponent's wheel in a carefully judged collision. It needed skilful driving and an iron nerve to complete the required seven laps, but the rewards of success were great. Diocles, the most famous of all charioteers, retired a millionaire and a national hero.

Circus racing was dangerous, but it was a true sport. The object was to win, not to maim or kill. No such excuse could be made for the gladiatorial shows to which the Roman mob was equally addicted. Gladiatorial conflict had arisen from the custom of setting a few slaves to fight over the grave of a dead nobleman, but by the first century B.C. the Roman people had become so depraved and eager for blood that no politician could hope to gain votes unless he staged a combat.

For many years the gladiators battled in the Circus Maximus or in some improvised arena. The first stone amphitheatre was constructed in 29 B.C. After its destruction in the great fire of A.D. 64, it was rebuilt as the now famous Colosseum. In its final form the Colosseum could seat 45,000 people and had standing room for another 5,000, but despite its size it was always packed during a show.

The Romans seemed insatiable in their thirst for blood. Under their relentless gaze men were pitted against men, hunters pursued and cut down their animal prey, while bound and helpless criminals were torn limb from limb by starving beasts. Human death could even be treated as a joke. Blindfolded convicts were pushed into the arena to cut and hack wildly at invisible opponents, while the crowd roared with laughter and shouted misleading advice. On a single day during the inauguration of the Colosseum in A.D. 80 five thousand animals were slaughtered. The stream of victims, human and non-human, continued to flow until the beginning of the fifth century A.D., when the games were at last suppressed by the Christian Emperor Honorius.

A gladiatorial show started with a parade of the fighters, splendidly dressed in purple and gold and followed by servants carrying their armour and weapons. Opposite the Imperial box the gladiators would halt, raise their arms, and shout in unison: "Hail Caesar, those who are about to die salute you." With this formality over, the serious business of fighting could commence.

To give variety there were several different types of gladiator. Samnites carried sword and shield, while Thracians had a round shield and a 139 dagger. Murmillones, who wore heavy armour and helmet, were usually matched against unarmoured Retiarii wielding net and trident. Production was slick. The crowd would not be kept waiting. When a gladiator fell, attendants dressed to resemble messengers of death raced out, struck the dying man on the forehead with a hammer to finish him off, and then dragged the corpse unceremoniously out of the arena. Occasionally a wounded gladiator might receive mercy. As the victor stood poised over his helpless adversary, he would glance up at the Emperor. If it had been a particularly even fight, the mob would yell for clemency, and the imperial thumb would turn upwards. The defeated gladiator would be spared to fight another day, and everyone would feel a warm glow of moral satisfaction. If thwarted by a poor performance, however, the audience would callously shriek, "Iugula" – "Butcher him." Without a qualm the Emperor would turn down his thumb, and another life would be gasped out on the blood-stained sand of the arena.

Bronze figure of a Roman gladiator.

Romans did, of course, follow other more innocent pastimes. Libraries and lectures catered for the intellectually inclined, while the many bars provided for those who wanted convivial company. Everyone went to the luxurious public baths, which the emperors had lavished on their subjects. It cost practically nothing to get in, but the baths offered far more than the opportunity for a good wash. They contained fullsize swimming pools, pleasant cafés, fine statues, and sometimes even a library. The baths became the great social centres of Rome and the colonial cities that aped its ways.

Constantinople inherited the Roman love for the baths and for chariot racing, but was protected from the degradation of gladiatorial contests by the disapproval of its Christian rulers. The Hippodrome, Constantinople's great stadium, could seat forty thousand people, all admitted free, but besides the chariot racing for which it was built the shows were mainly harmless displays of skill or daring similar to the acts in a modern circus. Chariot racing held such an appeal for the Byzantines that they sometimes decorated even the rare and costly silks, which came to them overland all the way from China, with Hippodrome scenes.

China was itself at that time a land of populous cities, but its townsmen enjoyed no free shows or races. Instead they had to work long and hard and endure the bullying of petty officials. Even during their scanty free time the ordinary Chinese were hemmed in by regulations. The police enforced a curfew, which prevented any organized entertainment after nightfall. Only on feast days, when the curfew was relaxed, did the people have a fleeting opportunity to enjoy themselves. Ch'ang-an, made capital once more in A.D. 582 after a long fall from favour, celebrated the lunar new year by closing down businesses and declaring a series of public holidays. Records have come down of a particularly spectacular "feast of the lanterns," celebrated in A.D. 713. A great structure, allegedly hung with 50,000 lanterns, was put up outside the emperor's palace, girls danced in the streets, and all Ch'ang-an echoed to the sound of merry-making until long after dark.

More than 550 years later, when Marco Polo visited China, the curfew was still in force, but city life was much more pleasurable. In fact, Polo, as a medieval Westerner, was profoundly impressed by the more advanced civilization he discovered in the East. When he finally returned home his fellow Venetians found his eye-witness accounts of city luxuries so incredible that they nicknamed him "Il Milione" because they insisted he had told them a million lies. Marco's description of Kinsai sounded just too good to be true. According to him the city had three thousand public

An illustration of bear-baiting from a mid-fourteenth century manuscript.

bath-houses to indulge its inhabitants in their whim for cold dips. If the weather had been warm and the baths had not refreshed them sufficiently, the citizens could rent a punt and glide gently over the waters of a beautiful local lake. For those who preferred dry land there were numerous pleasure gardens, which catered for customers who arrived in hired carriages. Even allowing for "Il Milione's" exaggeration, a picture remains of a city of great charm and gaiety.

The townsmen of Marco Polo's Europe could not rival their Chinese contemporaries in sophistication, but in their rougher way they amused themselves equally well. There were plenty of holidays. Every Sunday was free, and a document of 1474 relating to the English building trades recognized thirty-seven feastdays as whole or part holidays. People got up early, but their work finished at three or four o'clock in the afternoon, so that some free time remained before night fell and curfew restrictions forced them indoors. The Industrial Revolution robbed townsmen of most of their leisure, and it is only comparatively recently that they have begun to win it back.

Many medieval recreations were unruly or downright cruel. Boys and young men careered through the lanes playing football, and woe betide anyone who got in the way. Inquest records attest the not infrequent mortalities. The game was officially banned from the streets of London in 1314, but such was its appeal that no town could do more than temporarily suppress it. Military sports were also popular. William Fitzstephen writing in the twelfth century tells that on summer feastdays the young men of London went into the fields outside the walls to amuse themselves with "leaping, shooting with the bow, wrestling, casting the stone, playing with the ball, and fighting with their shields."

142

The same author makes all too clear the general pleasure that medieval townsmen took in cruelty to animals. On the morning of a winter holiday Londoners traditionally flocked to see boars slashing and goring one another with their tusks or to watch bulls and bears being baited by specially trained dogs. Spring was the season for cockfighting. "Every year," says Fitzstephen, "on the morning of Shrove Tuesday, the schoolboys of the city of London bring game cocks to their masters and in the fore part of the day, till dinner time, they are permitted to amuse themselves with seeing them fight."

But not all medieval pastimes were so brutal. The people loved to dance. Fitzstephen records that the girls of twelfth-century London danced away their summer holidays, and stopped only when it was too dark to go on. Often a dance would start spontaneously in a tavern, but even after the Sunday service it was not unknown for the congregation to let off steam with a joyous jig around the churchyard.

There were also professional entertainers who scraped a living by wandering across Europe, telling their stories, singing their songs, or performing feats of juggling and acrobatics wherever crowds gathered. The Church frowned on such showmen, and produced a rival attraction in the form of mystery plays. At Easter it had become the custom to add meaning to the services by having a few priests act out scenes from Christ's life. These dramas widened in scope and cast, outgrew the church, and moved out into the streets where they were performed on makeshift stages. All sorts of stories were told, ranging from biblical episodes to the sufferings of the martyrs. One play performed in London in 1409 even tried to portray the whole of the New and Old Testament. Not surprisingly it lasted for eight days. In all these religious plays light relief was supplied by devils who capered about in hideous masks and stole the serious actors' thunder.

As time passed many of the more sophisticated pleasures enjoyed by today's city-dwellers began to appear. Changing religious attitudes made the old mystery plays seem acts of blasphemy. Bishop Bonner of London banned their performance in any church in his diocese in 1542. Serious theatre had severed its connection with the Church, and a new line of development became possible. Before the end of the sixteenth century secular theatres had sprung up all over Europe. Italy led the movement, but other nations were not far behind. Germany's first theatre was a disused church in Nuremberg, converted in the 1550s. By 1579 Madrid had a theatre, while London's first playhouse was built in 1576 by James Burbage.

An engraving of Southwark, London showing the Bear Garden (left) and the Globe Theatre (right).

Although Burbage's theatre had to be built outside the city boundaries because of opposition from the puritanical authorities, Londoners flocked out to see the show. Several more theatres, amongst them the famous Globe, shot up in response to the enthusiasm for this new entertainment. The Globe, where Shakespeare himself acted in many of his own plays, was built in 1599, and was a typical English theatre of its day. A central unroofed yard was surrounded by galleries. It cost a penny to stand around the stage in the yard and two pence to sit in the gallery. If you wanted a cushion it was a penny extra.

Since Shakespeare's time Western theatre has enjoyed an uninterrupted history and has been carried to every corner of the world where Europeans have settled. In North America plays were given in makeshift surroundings long before the first permanent theatres were established in the eighteenth century. The Williamsburg playhouse, erected in about 1716, was the earliest in Colonial America. Charleston built one during the 1730s, followed a decade or so later by Philadelphia, but as late as 1750 New York's only theatre was a temporary structure. Nowadays, of course, New York has more than caught up. It has become one of the great entertainment centres of the world, and Broadway alone has thirty-five theatres.

Present-day musical entertainments have their origin in the Renaissance, just as does modern theatre. The plays with music which were to grow into opera started in the palaces of late-sixteenth-century Florence in Italy.

Interest in the new art form permeated down from the nobility, and the first opera house open to the general public was built in Venice in 1637. Milan's La Scala, the world's most famous opera house, was originally built in 1778, but owes its present form to the extensive reconstruction of 1946, which followed severe war damage.

Concert music has a slightly later origin. During the seventeenth century it became the custom for wealthy city-dwellers to invite their friends to a musical evening given by expert musicians. As far as is known the first time that money was charged for entry was in 1672, when the violinist John Bannister gave a recital in his London home. Concerts were given in eighteenth-century pleasure gardens, but it was not until the nineteenth century that classical music began to appeal to a wider audience. Most of the large concert halls which decorate the world's great cities were built in the twentieth century.

Parks are another feature of modern cities. Medieval townsmen could easily escape into the nearby countryside, but as cities grew their inhabitants found themselves more and more hemmed in by buildings, and less able to find any open spaces in which to relax. During the seventeenth and eighteenth centuries most city people resorted to private pleasure gardens for exercise and amusement, although generous kings like Charles I, who opened London's Hyde Park to the public in about 1635, were beginning to allow their subjects access to royal lands. Private gardens charged a modest entrance fee and offered pleasant surroundings in which their customers could stroll or sit down for an open-air meal. New attractions were added during the eighteenth century. In 1760 London's famous Vauxhall Gardens advertised continuous music from seven till ten in the evening, while its American counterpart, the New Vauxhall Gardens at Charleston, started musical recitals in 1767. Another famous London garden, Ranelagh, specialized in spectacular firework displays.

Open spaces and leisure were alike denied to the inhabitants of the unplanned industrial cities of the early nineteenth century. Houses huddled close around factories which were seldom idle. Since the Middle Ages free time had slowly been eroded away as employers became more demanding. By about 1830, at the height of the Industrial Revolution, the only holidays recognized in Britain were Sundays, Christmas Day and Good Friday.

Confined in their insanitary towns with virtually no relaxation except drink, factory operatives lived miserably deprived lives. Public conscience was finally aroused and governments began to acquire land for use as parks, so that industrial workers could escape, if only briefly, from the machines. In 1848 the British Parliament passed an act for the purchase

The Drive, Central Park, New York in 1895.

of land for "public walks." Other nations established similar measures, and today there is scarcely a city in the world without its park.

The nineteenth-century parks were essentially grassy open spaces with a few trees, where a person could enjoy a walk away from the crowded streets. In the more important parks there might be a bandstand, but that was usually the limit of the entertainment offered.

Modern parks, though retaining the grass and trees, provide many more facilities. Often there are tennis courts, bowling greens, and miniature golf courses as well as swings and slides for the children, while more occasionally there is a boating lake, a swimming pool, or sometimes even a cultural centre. Central Park in New York, whose 840 acres were laid out in the 1850s, has both a theatre and an area set aside for open air concerts.

A flourishing theatre had been one of the sparkling achievements of the Renaissance, but human progress is never even and while townsmen learned to appreciate majestic drama they continued to savour the sadistic pastimes of their ancestors. The Renaissance scholar Erasmus on a visit to the England of Henry VIII recorded that there were "many herds of bears maintained in this country for the purpose of baiting," and some years later Henry's daughter, Queen Elizabeth I, could be amused by what was called "a grand bear-beating." In Elizabeth's reign the London suburb of Southwark possessed two bear gardens where addicts would resort to watch the chained bears tormented by dogs or simply whipped by a number of men. On one occasion, however, the bears had the last laugh. During a Sunday afternoon performance in 1582 the spectator stands collapsed, killing and injuring many of those who a moment before had been eagerly following the sufferings of the dumb beasts.

Bull- and bear-baiting and cock fighting still attracted crowds in the early nineteenth century, but by this time civilized opinion had turned against them. Britain banned baiting in 1822, but further laws were needed in the 1830s before the distasteful practice was finally put down. Cock fighting could easily be staged in secret and was much harder to suppress.

Even before bull- and bear-baiting were finally outlawed, these so called sports had begun to lose ground to a new spectacle, the prize fight, which had developed into a crowd puller in eighteenth-century England. Prize fighting started with free-for-all contests between local champions whose supporters bet heavily on their hero's success. By 1719 there was a recognized champion of England, James Figg. Bare knuckle fighting, however, remained mainly an English sport until well into the nineteenth

A crowd of 90,000 watching baseball in Los Angeles.

century, and although an American champion was recognized in 1816, boxing did not become big business in the United States until after the Civil War. Thereafter it began to attract larger audiences, especially after the Queensberry Rules of 1867 won acceptance and removed much of the brawling element from the game.

Other great spectator sports developed in the late nineteenth century. From small beginnings in England during the 1870s soccer has grown into the most widely watched team game in the world. Most sizable towns in the United Kingdom have at least one professional soccer team and about a million Britons attend the Saturday matches. In many other countries the game is equally popular. The United States favours its own brand of football, which was played professionally in the 1890s, but did not attract large audiences until the 1920s. The other major spectator sport of American cities is baseball. A fee was first charged for entry to a game in 1858, and the sport grew rapidly after the 1870s.

The close of the nineteenth century also witnessed the beginnings of an entirely new form of entertainment, motion pictures, which were first shown to the public in Paris during 1895. Films became immensely popular. They were screened in music halls, at fair grounds, and even in converted shops, before specially designed cinemas made an appearance. Britain's first cinema, the Balham Empire in London, was not built until 1907, but such was the public demand that seven years later the country had more than four thousand. The cinema remained the premier entertainment medium until television began to reach a wider audience in the late '40s. Since then the number of cinemas has declined sharply, and many existing buildings have been converted into bingo halls or bowling alleys.

Over the five thousand years for which cities have existed their inhabitants' search for entertainment has led them to soaring achievements in drama and music as well as to the depths of cruelty and brutality. Today's city dwellers have a greater choice of pastime than ever before. They can watch or participate in many sports, or enjoy live performances in the theatre, opera house, and concert hall. A visit to the cinema still provides a night out in many suburbs, while those who prefer to stay at home can use television to bring the whole world into their own living-rooms.

10

City Government

Many facets of town life are today controlled by local city governments. Elected representatives in each town can voice the citizens' views on matters of common concern or their dissatisfaction with inadequate services. This has not always been so. Democratic self-government is a privilege which cities exercised in their beginnings but which in the course of history has often been lost to tyrants of one sort or another.

If the evidence of ancient stories has been correctly interpreted, Sumerian cities were true democracies during their formative period. Legends, which were already old when the scribes first wrote them down early in the second millennium B.C., refer to a divine assembly attended by all the gods, greater and lesser alike. Almost certainly such stories enshrined memories of a distant past when the entire adult population of a town gathered together to discuss public business.

These primitive democracies were killed primarily by the wars which arose towards the end of the fourth millennium B.C. from trading rivalries and squabbles over water rights. War conditions needed a single accepted leader, so the city assembly surrendered control to a "Lugal" or "Big Man" whose powers were meant to lapse once the crisis had passed. Inevitably the Lugal's temporary rule became permanent, and the importance of the assembly waned. Other influential officials also appeared at about the same time. An "Ensi" who supervised the city's fields was originally elected, but gradually managed to make his position hereditary. An "En," or high-priest, began to loom large in city affairs and usurp much of the former power of the assembly. When the offices of En and Lugal were fused and held by one person, the idea of kingship was born. Thereafter the cities of Sumeria succumbed to despotic rule, accepting the orders of the king or his appointed representative.

In Egypt a single ruler gained supremacy at an earlier stage than in Mesopotamia. Cities were still in their infancy when Egypt was unified in about 3200 B.C. by a warrior king who swept down from the south. There

An Egyptian official and his wife, seated statues
dating from the fourteenth century B.C.

Statue of Gudea, ensi of the Sumerian city of
Lagash.

could have been little opportunity for a tradition of urban democracy to become established before this conquest, and throughout almost the entire length of Egypt's long history the cities were, as seemed natural to their inhabitants, ruled over by representatives of the god-king, Pharaoh.

Although the towns of the Indus Valley were so well kept that their internal administration must have been extremely efficient, the form of government they employed remains a mystery. Some historians detect the shadow of a priest-king looming over each city from a citadel whose garrison was both a threat and a reassurance. Others, however, use the absence of great palaces, the fairly even distribution of wealth, and the obvious care for all sections of the population to support their theory that the cities were ruled by priestly oligarchies.

With the Greek cities the historian is on firmer ground. The Greek language and much of its literature have survived to give a vivid picture of developing city life and institutions. In Homeric times priest-kings, like Priam of Troy, were the dominant figures, but gradually authority passed to hereditary aristocracies. Oligarchic government gave way in some cities to a sort of democracy, but voting rights were never enjoyed by any but a small section of the population. In Athens, for example, Solon's constitution at the beginning of the sixth century B.C., while establishing an elected council of five hundred to control the city's affairs, gave the vote to only one Athenian in ten.

Cities swallowed by the power-hungry Roman Empire were initially treated differently according to how they were acquired. Italian towns which had allied themselves to Rome at the start of her career of conquest were allowed internal self-government, owing obedience to the central administration only in military and political matters. Other cities far-sighted enough to negotiate treaties with the expanding empire preserved certain rights as the reward for accepting Roman sovereignty. Some were spared tribute; some were granted municipal self-government. Most cities, however, were taken by force of arms, and these were put under the control of a Roman prefect, who extorted an annual tribute. After a territory had been overrun new cities were sometimes founded by veterans. Such colonies were allowed a considerable amount of autonomy.

The central government must have found its dealings with the cities of the Empire greatly complicated by the different status each enjoyed. Gradually distinctions began to disappear. Towns which had been subjected perhaps a hundred years earlier could hardly be treated as freshly vanquished foes. Claudius started to confer Roman citizenship on provincials during the first century A.D., and finally Caracalla, who ruled

Royal officers presenting a charter to a medieval city commune.

from A.D. 211–217, granted citizenship to all free inhabitants of the Empire. This was not an unmixed blessing, for some cities lost their privileged positions, and all became liable to imperial taxes.

Self-governing Roman cities were usually administered by municipal senates of one hundred life-members, mostly recruited from ex-magistrates. A portion of the revenue from market fees, fines, and communal property was set aside by the senate for the upkeep of their city. Water supplies, sewers, and theatres were provided at public expense, and the amenities of town life reached a degree of perfection not again rivalled until the nineteenth century.

As the Empire fell into decline, however, it became increasingly difficult to maintain standards, and the responsibilities of municipal government grew more and more burdensome. In areas where Christianity had come into prominence, the civil authorities surrendered their powers to the clergy, and many years went by before townsmen regained control of their affairs.

During the eleventh century there was a revival of city life in southern and central Europe and a resurgence of the spirit of independence. By banding together, guilds of townsmen gained sufficient strength to challenge successfully the authority of their ecclesiastical and feudal overlords. The towns of Northern Italy were the leaders in this movement, becoming virtual city-states each with its own foreign, as well as internal, policy. Milan was self-governing by 1093; seven years later so was Genoa. Government in the new republics rested on a broadly popular basis. Each city was administered by a number of consuls supported by an inner council, but all citizens were free to join in the general assembly. Later the consuls were replaced by a single executive officer, whose term of office was sometimes limited to as little as six months to prevent him gaining too much personal power and influence. Inevitably, however, certain families advanced in wealth and importance, so that by the fourteenth century the rise of aristocratic clans had seriously weakened the democratic fabric of society. The process culminated in the city monarchies of the sixteenth century.

Only in Germany and the Low Countries, and along the Baltic Sea coast did other cities gain such complete liberty to pursue their own internal and external affairs. The few large German towns which had existed before the tenth century had been under the sway of either a bishop or duke, but gradually more freedom was won by the concerted action of guilds of citizens. To protect their hard-won privileges, cities began to ally themselves together. The most important combination, the Hanseatic League, arose from the mutual protection treaty made in 1241 between Lübeck and Hamburg. The league eventually grew to embrace seventy Baltic and Low Country towns, and had its own central council, treasury, and army, but within this structure each member city remained autonomous in its internal government.

Hanseatic towns were controlled by their guilds. The usual arrangement was for a large council to make general policy decisions, which were then implemented by a smaller executive group. All town officials were appointed by the various guilds, but the most influential positions generally went to the more prosperous merchants. The freedom of the Hanseatic cities lasted until they were engulfed by the rising tide of nationalism, which swept Europe in the sixteenth century.

The influence of the Italian republics was strongly felt in southern France, but although such cities as Arles, Avignon, and Marseilles formed consular governments during the twelfth century, they were unable to win the complete freedom of action enjoyed by their mentors. Farther to

The Hanseatic town hall at Brunswick, Germany.

the north, away from the centres of democracy, the grip of the feudal lords proved harder to break. Townsmen in northern France secured certain rights by acting together in trade guilds or sometimes in religious societies, but they never completely succeeded in shaking off the hand of external authority. During the twelfth century, when Henry II of England controlled Normandy, Maine, and Poitou, that imperious ruler personally appointed many of the "maires" of towns lying within his territory. As the French monarchy itself grew stronger in the thirteenth and fourteenth centuries, it extended a steadily growing influence over those towns which had gained a measure of independence. The shadow of excessive central power still lies over French municipal government in the twentieth century.

English cities nearly all started on the road to municipal freedom by negotiating monetary treaties with the crown. The process originated as far back as Saxon times when the citizens of certain towns bought exemption from individual tolls and tariffs by agreeing to pay, as a group, a fixed annual fee to the king. Usually collection was left in the hands of the local sheriff, who inevitably attempted to extort more than was really due so that he could keep a portion for himself. It was greatly to a town's advantage if its inhabitants could persuade the king to do away with this intermediary and instead accept a direct payment. The acquisition of this 155 right was a major step towards real self-government. The officials chosen to gather the money acted on behalf of their own community rather than as agents of outside authority.

Until the thirteenth century English city government contained a strong element of democracy. All freemen had a voice in the assembly and a vote in the annual election of town officers. It was only when the growth of population made a full meeting of freemen unwieldy, that committees of twelve or twenty-four members began to appear to manage town affairs. The importance of the assembly of freemen diminished once such a committee was formed, and although annual elections often continued they became mere matters of form, allowing the same wealthy citizens to hold office for term after term. In many places the decay of the democratic principle had become so complete by the fifteenth century that the authority of self-perpetuating oligarchies was never seriously challenged.

As English towns drifted inexorably towards oligarchy, a pattern of municipal government evolved which was accepted over most of the country. At the head of the administration the mayor combined the functions of chief executive and principal magistrate. Beneath him came the aldermen, who represented the various wards of the city and who served as assistant magistrates. Finally there was a common council, in theory elected each year, but often appointed by the ruling clique.

The Tudor dynasty, which rose to power late in the fifteenth century and maintained its position until Queen Elizabeth I died childless in 1603, favoured oligarchic municipalities as part of its policy of strong central government. Small groups of men with a lot to lose were much more susceptible to royal control than large democratic organizations would have been. Many new town charters were granted by the crown at this time to give oligarchies the full backing of the law. Mayor and council, initially appointed by name, were given the right to elect their own successors. Such legally constituted corporations had the privilege of sending members to Parliament, so by one astute move the monarch secured both a Parliamentary majority and the loyalty of many important towns. Closed, self-perpetuating corporations ruled most English cities until a measure of democracy was re-introduced by the passage of the Municipal Corporations Act in 1835.

The rise of strong national states in France and Spain at the close of the Middle Ages had the effect of reducing what municipal democracy existed in these countries. Even Paris had little say in its own affairs, and the gradual improvements in such things as its water supply, lighting, and policing were due to decisions taken by the central government. A modicum of self-rule was secured by some French towns, whose citizens clubbed together to buy the municipal posts offered for sale by Louis XIV in and after 1692, but even such enterprising places remained under tight state control.

In England the closed municipal oligarchies, brought into existence centuries before for political ends, presided helplessly over the explosive surge of urban growth which coincided with the Industrial Revolution. As early as the reign of George II (1727–60) the wealthier cities found it necessary to step outside the municipal structure and approach Parliament for special improvement acts conferring the right to levy local rates to finance street paving, cleansing, and lighting. Often these new powers were given to specially created boards of commissioners rather than entrusted to the existing corrupt administrations. This produced such a chaos of conflicting authorities that more time was wasted in argument than employed in useful work.

A rising tide of anger at the way towns were governed led in 1835 to a Parliamentary investigation of municipal corporations. Out of the 212 towns scrutinized, 186 had self-electing governments making absolutely no pretence at democracy. Even in the towns which held elections, only the freemen, who numbered on average something like one in twenty of the inhabitants, could vote. Municipal corruption was rife and city funds were frequently misapplied.

The Municipal Corporations Act of the same year, 1835, reformed the city governments of England and Wales and put them on a more democratic footing. The old titles of mayor, alderman, and councillor survived, but such worthies were no longer allowed to vote themselves into indefinite office. Instead the rate-payers elected councillors to serve for three years. The representative town councils formed in this way did, however, retain the right to appoint their own mayors and aldermen without further reference to the electorate. Mayors held office for a single year, aldermen for six.

The structure of city government in Colonial America was similar to eighteenth-century English practice, but with one vital difference. There was an element of democracy. The mayor was normally appointed by the provincial governor, but the councilmen and sometimes even the aldermen were elected by local residents of good standing. Only three cities, Annapolis, Norfolk, and Philadelphia, had closed, self-perpetuating corporations.

Even these few city oligarchies did not long survive the War of Independence. In 1787 the Virginia State legislature passed an act condemning

Eighteen-year-olds can now vote in British civic elections.

"the former method of electing common councilmen for the borough of Norfolk . , . [as] . . . impolitic and unconstitutional." Two years later Philadelphia swung over to popular election, confirming city democracy as accepted United States practice. The democracy was not a complete one, however, because property qualifications of some kind were required to secure a vote. Outside influence was also felt from the state legislatures, which had taken over the Colonial governors' old prerogative of appointing the mayors of towns within their jurisdiction.

During the first half of the nineteenth century both these impediments to full local democracy were largely removed. By 1850 property qualifications for municipal suffrage had almost vanished, while it was increasingly common for the mayor to be voted into office by his fellow townsmen instead of appointed from above. Boston, Detroit, Philadelphia, and St Louis all elected their own mayors by the 1820s and in the course of the next decade Baltimore and New York won the same right.

Coupled with these advances came an extension of municipal activity necessitated by rapid urban expansion. The mid-nineteenth century population of New York City had topped the half-million mark, Philadelphia was not far behind, and Boston and Baltimore each had 200,000 inhabitants. Somehow law and order had to be enforced, and reasonable amenities provided in these already huge and fast-growing communities. Water supply, sewering, and road building could no longer be left to the vagaries of public spirited self-help. Town authorities had to step in and take on new responsibilities whether they liked it or not.

New York's municipality set the pace in the United States. Its Croton aqueduct was completed in 1842, while its police service, established in 1845, was the first major force in America. Other United States cities began to follow New York's example. Boston started the construction of the Cochituate waterworks in 1846; Chicago and Baltimore had municipal water supplied by the 1850s. This enlargement of the scope of civic responsibilities was not, of course, confined to the United States. It was paralleled and to some extent anticipated by similar events in Europe, where the Industrial Revolution had shaken city administrations out of their age-old absorption with trading concessions. The whole urban environment was becoming the concern of municipal government.

Modern America has two main types of city administration. Many large communities hold a city-wide election for mayor, while individual wards each elect their own representatives to serve on the town council. Usually the mayor is a dominant figure with control over finance, and the power both to veto council decisions and to appoint or dismiss officials. Some

Cleveland, U.S.A. elects a mayor.

smaller towns elect councils to frame general policies, but leave the day-to-day running of their affairs to a professional city manager.

The forms of government are different in other nations, but everywhere the same awe-inspiring responsibilities have to be faced. Urbanization is advancing all over the world, and the conditions in which future generations live will be largely determined by the quality of city government.

11

City Planning

By the end of the twentieth century the world's urban population will be four times greater than it is today. One hundred years from now the tentacles stretching out from traditional city centres will form an interlocking mesh covering perhaps a third of the earth's land area. The whole world will be one city. Unless the environment is carefully planned, life in the future could lapse into a nightmare, compared with which the conditions in our own sprawling, traffic-choked towns would seem idyllic. The random city growth accepted in the past can no longer be tolerated in the age of population explosion. Urban planning has become a necessity.

The first town planners were the ancient people of the Indus Valley. Many succeeding civilizations have discovered the same art in the four thousand years since Mohenjo-daro and Harappā were laid out, but planned towns still remain a rarity. Most cities grow slowly and haphazardly through the efforts of generations of inhabitants. It is only when an already advanced civilization founds new settlements that urban planning has a chance to appear.

Ancient Egypt is a case in point. The greater cities of the land were allowed to add to themselves, higgledy-piggledy as social and economic forces dictated. Planning was confined to certain minor places built for special purposes. The fortified towns, established at the beginning of the second millennium B.C. to protect the southern approaches to Egypt at the Second Cataract, had straight streets laid out with military precision. Order was also imposed on pyramid-cities like the one at Kahun put up in the nineteenth century B.C. to house workers constructing and later maintaining the tomb of Sesostris II. Hotep Sesostris, as this town was called, was enclosed by a rectangular mud-brick rampart and divided into two unequal segments by an interior wall running north to south. Segregated in the smaller western section, the unskilled labourers were crammed into row on row of identical houses ranged along a series of straight main roads. The more spacious residential area reserved for officials had larger   161

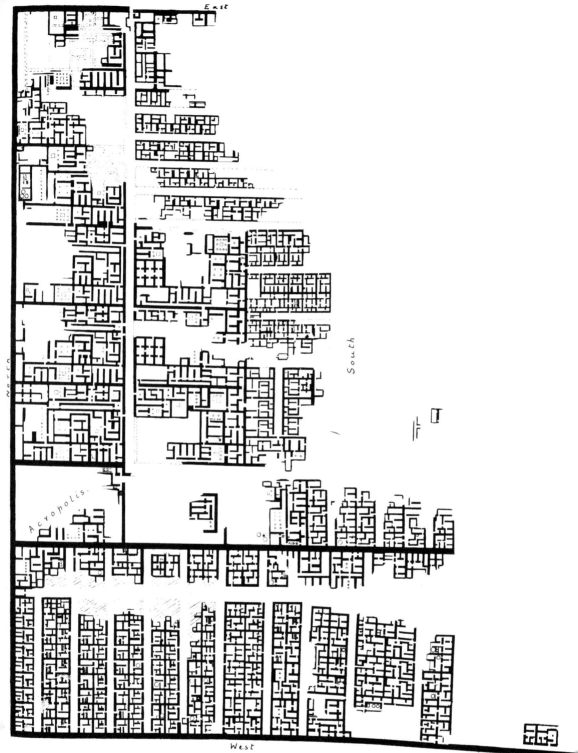

Plan of the Egyptian Pyramid city at Kahun, nineteenth century B.C.

162

homes, but a similar well-planned street system.

In the Greek world of fifteen hundred years later there was again a clear distinction between old cities which had evolved slowly over the ages and new towns laid out to pre-conceived plans. Greek planning was a by-product of the war waged against Persia. This desperate conflict arising from Persian expansion left many of the Greek colonies of Asia Minor in ruins, but provided them with the chance to make a fresh start. Miletus, which was destroyed in 494 B.C. and rebuilt soon after the final defeat of the Persians in 479 B.C., was probably the first Greek city to have a regular grid of streets. One of its sons, Hippodamus, who became the most important figure in Greek town planning, was born in about 480 B.C. He must have owed much of the inspiration for his later teachings on the advantages of broad straight streets and the beauty of harmoniously grouped buildings to a boyhood spent amongst the scenes of reconstruction.

In adult life Hippodamus moved to Athens, but although his ideas won wide respect there was little he could do to improve the old-established cities of mainland Greece. Only demolition on an unthinkable scale could have imposed order on their crooked lanes. Many cities, like Athens itself, were content to relieve the squalor of their tortuous alleys with fine public buildings. Sparta did not even bother to do that. Secure in its military prestige, it scorned any adornment of its winding, filth-strewn streets.

Hippodamus' chances came when his Athenian hosts founded new cities. In about 450 B.C. he was entrusted with the design of the Piraeus, the port of Athens, and laid it out with broad, straight streets. Another opportunity occurred when the Athenians established their colony of Thurii in southern Italy.

The chessboard street pattern championed by Hippodamus enabled building plots to be easily defined, besides conferring on the planned city a new dignity and order. Greek towns were usually small and almost free from wheeled vehicles, so that the main disadvantages of the grid system, monotony and traffic snarl-ups at street junctions, did not reveal themselves.

Alexander's conquests of the latter half of the fourth century B.C. opened up a vast area for Greek exploitation. Greek-style towns were founded all over western Asia, and the Hippodamian method came into its own. It is known from ancient writings that Alexander's own city of Alexandria was laid out chessboard fashion, with one great road, Canopic Street, stretching in an unbroken line for some four miles. The symmetry of Alexandria must have been copied on a smaller scale by many lesser cities.

Priene, built on the east coast of the Aegean late in the fourth century B.C., is a well excavated example of a planned city of Alexander's time. Although the site, on a southward facing slope, did not invite regularity, a grid pattern was strictly applied. There was no pretension or conscious straining after grandeur, but the contrast between the main streets running level along the contours and the steep side streets rising in steps up the hillside must have been very pleasing. Near the centre of the town was the colonnaded agora, the only open space within the built-up area. This was flanked by a temple and other major buildings, while the four hundred private houses were distributed along the surrounding grid of streets. In its prime Priene's population probably numbered about four thousand.

Most Hellenistic towns were, like Priene, planned for comfort and convenience rather than for spectacular effects. The rise of powerful national states had curtailed the independence of cities, so that public buildings as symbols of civic unity no longer held the importance they had once possessed. Only in the capitals of the empires, which had been carved out by Alexander's successors, was there much striving towards splendour. Pergamon, as the seat of the Attalid kings, was obviously designed to impress. During the third and second centuries B.C. the steep hill which dominated the town was crowned with an arc of stately build-ings. On the highest part of the ridge stood the palace, next came the famous library, then temples to Athena, Zeus, and Dionysus. Below, cut into the rock of the hillside was a beautiful theatre. But with all this care lavished on the state buildings, so little was left for the ordinary town that it developed in unplanned squalor. Given a chance the citizens of Pergamon might well have sacrificed some of the glories of their public architecture for a little of the comfort and order of a much humbler town.

Roman town planning probably owed much to Greek example, but it was also influenced by native traditions. From time immemorial the Roman augurs, who attempted to foretell the future by interpreting bird flight and other natural signs, had divided the universe into four quarters by marking out right-angled lines on the ground with their staffs of office. Land commissioners followed this hallowed precedent, and parcelled out territory by drawing two guide lines, which with further parallel lines split an area into a number of neat rectangular units.

Planning was, therefore, not alien to the Roman mind, but Rome itself evolved too quickly to be controlled. It was already a substantial city before its inhabitants were advanced enough to appreciate the benefits of broad streets and a regular layout. Like the cities of mainland Greece, Rome's many splendid buildings only emphasized the general chaos of its streets. The Romans' developing taste for symmetry had to find expression in the colonies rather than in the mother city.

Pompeii, destined to be engulfed by an eruption of Vesuvius, marked a half-way stage in Roman town planning. It was re-founded in 80 B.C. as a colony for veterans from Sulla's army, and most of the roadways subsequently buried and preserved beneath volcanic ash must have been set out at this time. The town plan as revealed by excavation shows many straight streets, but an overall pattern was lacking. Later Roman foundations became far more regular as Greek influence grew stronger. Roman custom was refined by Hippodamian theory.

Traces of ancient chessboard layouts can sometimes be discerned in the alignment of the older streets of Italian towns which have survived from Roman into modern times. In Turin, founded by Augustus in about 28 B.C. as Augusta Taurinorum, Roman road metalling has been discovered beneath certain present-day streets showing that the grid pattern is as old as the town itself. Piacenza, Bologna, Parma, Modena, and Florence likewise still preserve, in the criss-cross of their central streets, a reminder of the original symmetry of their ground plans.

The best preserved examples of later Roman town planning come, however, from colonies set in more distant provinces. North Africa, where some sites have lain deserted and undisturbed since the Roman occupation, has provided particularly valuable evidence. A picture has emerged of the typical provincial town surrounded by a rectangular wall and cut into four equal sections by the two principal streets which met at the central forum. Side streets crossing at right angles divided each quarter into convenient, rectangular building lots. Timgad, founded in A.D. 100 by the Emperor Trajan and long buried beneath the sands of Algeria before its discovery and excavation by French archaeologists, ran true to type.

The concept of the rectangle as the basis for setting out cities has arisen in other widely separated civilizations. In China a tradition of rectilinear planning extends back in time for perhaps three thousand years. Possibly it originated from the intrusion into the urban environment of the ancient country custom of dividing farm land into square units. By Han times (c.200 B.C. to c.A.D. 200) the ideal of the planned city was well established. The original Han capital of Ch'ang-an occupied a roughly rectangular area twenty-five kilometres in perimeter, and was encompassed by a mighty wall pierced by twelve gateways, three in each side. From the gates the city was traversed by a grid of straight streets which crossed one another at right angles. Such has been the continuity of Chinese culture that grid patterns can still be detected in the older parts of many existing

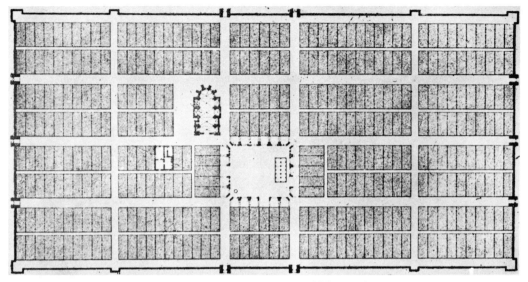

This plan of the thirteenth-century French town of Montpazier shows that not all medieval towns were chaotic.

towns.

Chessboard layouts were also a feature of some of the towns of pre-Columbian America. Teotihuacán itself, greatest of all the indigenous cities of Central America, conformed to a rigid grid over the whole of the eight square miles which it occupied at the height of its power in about A.D. 400. At some point early in the city's history a plan must have been established to integrate all further development. The chosen grid was based on the majestic ceremonial way now called the Street of the Dead, which started in the north below the huge mass of the Pyramid of the Moon and ran southwards through the city in an unbroken line for about six thousand metres. From the city centre, where the main road passed between the citadel and a probable market square, another great street extended arms to the east and west. All subsidiary streets paralleled one or the other of the main avenues, and most of the individual buildings followed the same orientation.

Most cities in medieval Europe were pitiful compared with the planned grandeur of central Teotihuacán. Nowhere amongst their narrow, crooked alleys was there a rival to the Street of the Dead. But although the majority of towns grew gradually and fitted houses into whatever space could be found within the walls, this was not always so. Some medieval towns were created artificially, and planned in their entirety. Often such towns were planned in freshly conquered areas for military reasons, but later some were founded as commercial ventures. A successful trading town was a rich source of tolls for the lord on whose land it was built. The thirteenth century, when new towns were established in their greatest numbers, 166 marked the high tide of medieval planning.

A complete Vitruvian town. Palma Nova, Italy from the air.

Town building slowed down after this, and interest in planning waned until re-awakened during the Renaissance by the wide circulation of a book written long before by the Roman architect Vitruvius. Carried along on the wave of enthusiasm for things classical, the architects of fifteenth-century Italy adopted this Roman devotee of the planned city as their guide and master.

Vitruvius saw the perfect town as completely circular with a forum acting as the hub from which the main roads radiated outwards. Lesser streets lay in a series of concentric rings about the central open space. Although the scheme was purely theoretical, and had never been tried out in ancient times, the Renaissance architects chose to ignore the practical disadvantage of curved building lots, because of the strong attraction they felt for the plan's symmetry and elegance. Many dream cities were sketched out on paper, but few planners got the chance to translate their thoughts into reality. The great period for the foundation of new towns had passed with the Middle Ages, so that opportunities were limited. One of the few truly Vitruvian towns was Palma Nova, the Venetian frontier post designed by Vincenzo Scamozzi in 1593.

Most architects had to suppress their wider aspirations and content themselves with beautifying existing streets rather than designing whole new towns. In these smaller schemes symmetry was still the prime objective. Uneven frontages and roofs at widely different heights were not tolerated. The street and its buildings were conceived as a harmonious whole, the cities where planners had been active took on a new stateliness. Rome, which had fallen on such evil times at the end of the Middle Ages that it was almost derelict, was largely reconstructed in the new style during the fifteenth and sixteenth centuries. There was no overall scheme for the city, but large sections were planned. The effect on Rome was, as the Popes had hoped, "to compel all to acknowledge her as the Capital of the World." Architects from all over Europe viewed her buildings with admiration, and her example did much to encourage the spread of Renaissance design into other countries.

France was the first nation apart from Italy to take up Vitruvian ideas, but once more improvements were generally limited to a few new streets superimposed on the chaotic cities inherited from medieval times.

Renaissance planning theories had little impact on other countries until the seventeenth century, when besides finding acceptance in Britain and Germany they bore fruit even in the distant American colonies. When William Penn founded Philadelphia in 1682, he chose to make it a planned city. Two main roads, which split the town into four parts, met at a

One of the elegant Georgian crescents in Bath, England.

An aerial picture showing the grid structure of New York's streets.

central open space, and each of the quarters was further sub-divided by streets meeting at a public garden.

England produced no completely planned cities in this period. Its towns were well established, and improvements were generally limited to new suburbs. Some of the streets added to London in the seventeenth and eighteenth centuries were set out in a pleasing and stately fashion, but it was Bath under the guiding hands of architect John Wood that became the jewel of English planning. Bath had come into vogue as a spa at the end of the seventeenth century, and during the eighteenth it was transformed and enlarged by a series of beautifully balanced streets and crescents.

The nineteenth century witnessed an unparalleled expansion in the size of cities. Factories needed workers, and workers needed houses. In town after town, first in Britain and then in Europe and the United States, row upon row of mean dwelling places were thrown up without consideration or thought. There were no parks, no amenities, just dreary streets of low grade houses.

The worst housing abuses were tackled in the nineteenth century itself. Minimum building standards were established, and parks were provided to lessen the gloom of industrial areas. Nothing was done, however, to limit town growth. Advances in public transport allowed the suburbs to be pushed out further and further from the old centre, destroying all feeling of city unity. William Morris, the British artist, reformer, and outspoken critic of the industrial age, voiced a growing disquiet when in a lecture of 1884 he attacked "the black horror and reckless squalor of our manufacturing districts" and the "wretched suburbs that sprawl all round our fairest and most ancient cities."

Eventually the ugliness of the industrial centres provoked a reaction. In Britain, where the workers' homes had perhaps been crowded together more shamefully than anywhere else, it took the form of the "garden city" movement led by Ebenezer Howard. Howard advocated the foundation of new, planned towns of predetermined size and low population density to rehouse people from the already over-bloated cities. His first town, Letchworth, founded in 1903, had at most only twelve houses to the acre, compared with the eighty not uncommon in city slums.

A new awareness of the need for real planning began to permeate the western world. The "city beautiful" movement, inspired by Utopian plans exhibited at the Chicago World's Fair of 1893, gathered strength in the United States and culminated in the Chicago improvement scheme of 1909. That year, 1909, marked a turning point for town planning. Not

Houses in the spacious new town of Harlow, England. New towns are Britain's major contribution to modern planning.

only was the Chicago project published, but America's very first planning conference was held, while the British Parliament passed a Housing and Town Planning Act.

If technological progress had not been so rapid, this upsurge of enthusiasm for planning might have achieved more than it did. In actual fact the advent of the motorcar changed the whole course of urban expansion. The nineteenth-century city had developed as a series of suburbs clustered along radial public transport routes reaching out from the old town nucleus. As the twentieth century progressed the car freed more people from dependence on trams and trains, and houses began to spread into the open country that had been left between the earlier radial routes. Sprawl was worse than ever, the countryside had retreated, and suburbanites' cars converging on the centre encountered mounting congestion. Before planners had a chance to come to terms with the city spawned by public transport, they were overwhelmed by that produced by the automobile.

Cities began to appoint planning departments only after most of the damage had been done. Given a new site a gifted designer can create a city as daring and beautiful as Brasilia, but the hands of a planner dealing with an established metropolis are largely tied. If he interferes with existing buildings he affects not just bricks and mortar but people's businesses, lives, and homes. Although planners may sometimes long to wipe the slate clean and start afresh, like the rest of us they have to live in cities we have inherited. They have practical plans to deal with the situation as they find it, and dreams of idealized cities for the more distant future.

Many planners have concentrated on improving transport so as to make the city centre more accessible from the suburbs. To ease vehicle movement America's cities have embarked on spectacular freeway programmes at enormous expense both in money and buildings demolished, only to find the gains fleeting. Improvements have swiftly been overtaken by the increased volume of traffic using the new highways, and the congestion relieved at one point has simply been transferred to another part of the town. So many people have been encouraged to drive to work that in some United States' city centres more land is devoted to roads, parking spaces, and garages than to shops and offices.

The point has been reached where the car is spoiling city life and somehow its increasing use must be checked. More and more, planners are turning their attention towards re-vitalising and extending public transport systems. Already many cities have closed a few of their streets to vehicles to make pedestrian precincts where shoppers may stroll at ease. Perhaps in the future cars will be completely excluded from central regions which will be served instead by new modes of public transport.

Britain has been less concerned with re-organizing urban transport than with trying to lessen the need for it. The central theme of modern British planning has been an attempt to limit the further expansion of the country's giant cities. Suburban sprawl has been partially checked by establishing green belts — zones where new building is restricted — around cities like London and Glasgow, while efforts have also been made to attract people away from the existing urban areas. Since the Second World War twenty-eight New Towns in the tradition of Howard's Garden Cities have been set up, and more are planned. Factories have been built as well as houses, so that these new communities could become real towns rather than commuter dormitories. In many ways the New Towns have been outstandingly successful. They offer an improved environment, and some, like Cumbernauld in Scotland, have won international acclaim. As the solution to the inexorable growth of the big cities, however, they have not come up to expectations.

America, too, has its New Towns, but as most have been founded within existing Metropolitan Areas they are often satellite dormitories rather than independent communities. Though care has been taken to locate churches, schools, community centres and homes in well planned, harmonious settings, the vital ingredient of local industry which would have changed such suburban developments into genuine New Towns has frequently been omitted. Park Forest, Illinois, begun in 1947, the Levit-towns of the late '40s and early '50s, and even the majority of the forty New Towns born out of a wave of enthusiasm during the 1960s share, for all their other attractions, this one fundamental weakness. In only a few, like Reston and Columbia, is there sufficient industry for citizens to find work within their own town.

But what of the future? How can continuing urban expansion be managed so as to produce an acceptable environment? The planners can parade a host of competing strategies for approval. Some envisage a world of vertical cities — great two-mile-high towers piling up the population instead of allowing it to spread thinly over the face of the earth. Others suggest linear cities each with a string of urban centres linked by one major transport route. Perhaps the most workable concept, however, is that of a stellar metropolis with a number of miniature linear cities extending out from a common city core. The core would have true urban character. In it would be located the major theatres, concert halls, museums, and places of higher education. The branches would have their own local

Victor Gruen's plan for the ideal metropolis shows ten cities linked to a central urban nucleus by radial communication routes.

centres for shopping and entertainment, and would be flanked on either side by open land. Plans for the development of Stockholm and Copenhagen are somewhat along these lines. If the predicted world city comes into existence, the arms of neighbouring stellar towns could be allowed to meet, but their inhabitants would retain easy access to the countryside.

Through this welter of conflicting plans and startling prophecies runs one common assumption: cities will continue to grow. Already many townspeople feel themselves lost amongst a crowd of uncaring strangers. In the world city of tomorrow the sense of alienation could be crushing unless the unending suburbs can be given some meaningful form. Planners must not simply concentrate on slick transportation schemes and spectacular effects; they must also ensure that each neighbourhood has its own character and sense of community. The future happiness of the bulk of mankind relies on the success of their efforts.

Highway planning gets top priority in Los Angeles which has more automobiles per person than any other city.

Acknowledgements

Acknowledgements are due to the following for permission to reproduce pictures on the pages indicated: Aerofilms, 3, 167; Alden Self-Transit Systems Corporation, 51; *American Scenery*, (1840), 71; Department of Archaeology, Pakistan, 4R; Museum of Archaeology and Ethnology, Cambridge, 55; Department of Architecture and Planning, City of Bath, 169; Photograph Ashmolean Museum, 111T; *The Bayeux Tapestry*, (Phaidon Press, 1957), 17; Curators of the Bodleian Library, 128/9; The Trustees of the British Museum, 5, 36, 37, 57, 62, 67, 110, 111B, 114, 133, 140, 142, 151R; Photograph by Byron, The Byron Collection, Museum of the City of New York, 25, 103, 131B, 146; Cia Mexicana Aerofoto, 10; Museum of Classical Archaeology, Cambridge, 134; Compagnie d'Energétique Linéaire mb, 54; Didron, *Annales Archéologiques*, (Paris, 1852), 166; W. B. Emery, *Archaic Egypt*, (Penguin Books, 1961), 6; Ford News Department, 119; Guiseppe Gatteschi, *Past and Present Rome*, (Peter Owen, 1956), 123; Greater London Council Print Collection, 130; Courtesy of the Victor Gruen Foundation for Environmental Planning, 175; Harlow Development Corporation, 172; Leeds City Library, 23; *Li Monumenti più celebri di Roma antica e moderna*, (Rome, 1850), 76; The London Museum, 68, 70, 81, 97; London Transport Board, 39, 46; Photograph by Los Angeles County Air Pollution Control District, 88; Louvre Museum, Paris, 90T, 151L; Courtesy of William Mangin, 29; Mansell-Alinari, 14; Mansell Collection, 22, 87, 96, 117, 124, 144; Merryweather & Sons Ltd., 106; Sir Ellis Minns, 90B; John W. Mott, City of Cleveland, 160; National Dairy Council, 131T; Courtesy of National Ocean Survey, National Oceanic and Atmospheric Administration, 170; National Tourist Organisation of Greece, London, 13, 135T; New York Fire Department, 107; *New York Illustrated*, (1881), 24, 49; Novosti Press Agency, 44; Courtesy of the Oriental Institute, University of Chicago, 4L, 32, 75L; Pace, 158; Pardoe, *Beauties of the Bosphorus*, (1861), 64; W. M. F. Petrie, *Illahun, Kahun & Gurob*, 162; Police Department, City of New York, 104; Director of Public

Health Engineering, Greater London Council, 83; Radio Times Hulton Picture Library, 102; Photograph by Paul Rice for the New York City Housing and Development Administration, 28; Brian Richards, *New Movement in Cities*, (Studio Vista, 1966), 52; Courtesy of Anthony Ridley, 19, 27, 72, 155; Photograph by Jacob A. Riis, The Jacob A. Riis Collection, Museum of the City of New York, 85; *Rome au Siècle d'Auguste*, 135B, 138; Photo P. Ronald, Exclusive Editions Arthaud, 34, 58; Copyright Bibliothèque Royale Albert Ier, Brussels, 125 (Ms 9066, f. 11 recto), 153 (Ms 9242, f. 274); Photo Science Museum, London, 42/3, 45, 48, 99, 100; Smithsonian Institution, 40; Andrew Tomko III, 120; Trinity College Library, Cambridge, 66; Turkish Tourist Information Office, London, 65; United States Information Service, 50, 132, 148, 176; George E. Waring, *Street Cleaning*, (Gay & Bird, 1898), 86; Courtesy of Sir Mortimer Wheeler, 8, 60, 75R; Sir Leonard Woolley, *Ur of the Chaldees*, (Benn, 1929), 12; Charles Young, *Fires, Fire Engines and Fire Brigades* (1866), 105.

Index

Figures in bold type denote pictures